The New and Revised Catalog of

American Collectibles

Maryanne O'Donnell

The New and Revised Catalog of American Collectibles

By William C. Ketchum, Jr. Photography by John Garetti

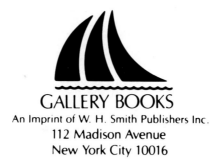

GALLERY BOOKS
An Imprint of W. H. Smith Publishers Inc.
112 Madison Avenue
New York City 10016

© 1979 by Mayflower Books, Inc., and Rutledge Books, Inc. All rights reserved.
Published by Gallery Books, a division of W.H. Smith, Inc., 112 Madison Avenue, New York, New York 10016.

Library of Congress Cataloging in Publication Data

Ketchum, William C 1931-
  The catalog of American collectibles.

  "A Rutledge/Mayflower book."
  Includes index.
  1. Americana—Catalogs. 2. Antiques—United States—Catalogs. I. Title.
NK805.K472   745.1'0973   79-12760
ISBN: 0-8317-6316-7

Printed in the United States of America

Third Printing, 1984

Contents

Introduction

In the early 1970s, some promoters of antiques shows began to advertise their extravaganzas as "antiques and collectibles" shows or even simply as "collectibles" shows. This was more than a change in language; it was a reflection of a fundamental alteration in the nature of both the collecting public and what it collected.

Before the Second World War, antiques buying was limited. An antique is legally defined by U.S. Customs as an object one hundred or more years old, so nothing later than 1850 was of much interest to most antiquarians. Furthermore, even among the older objects, much was left untouched. Collectors were for the most part rich, eccentric, or both, and they concentrated their efforts on a limited field: fine arts, furniture, silver, and certain glass and pottery. Those few who explored other areas of eighteenth- and nineteenth-century arts and crafts found low prices and little competition.

By 1950 all this had begun to change. A huge new class of collectors emerged during the postwar years—people who had never before had the time or the money to collect. Younger and more adventuresome than their predecessors, they

began to expand the concept of "antique." Scouring the country for old things, they discovered the "new" antiques: quilts, folk art, decorated stoneware pottery—even bottles. Much of what they acquired was truly antique in that it was a century or more old—so the older generation of collectors could quarrel with the younger collectors on aesthetic grounds but not on temporal ones. On the other hand, a lot was collected that everybody knew wasn't very old: hooked rugs from the turn of the century and country baskets from the 1930s. Still, these items were "folky," and everyone tacitly agreed to forget about age and call them antiques.

The source of this inspired reasoning was, to a great extent, the antiques dealer. Before the postwar boom, most antiques dealers had been people who sold to feed their own collecting habit. Few of them made much money, and few hoped to. Their rewards were of another kind. Suddenly, however, it became possible to make a living selling antiques. What had been a hobby became a business—a big business—and as more and more dealers entered the field, the demand for salable merchandise greatly increased. Dealers searched the countryside and even trav-

Fashion dolls; 1900–30; $70–285 each. Textile-covered boudoir lamp; 1920–30; $45–76.

eled to Canada and England—where American antiques (or things that looked like American antiques) could be obtained. But there was still not enough pre-1850 merchandise to go around. The only way out was to call things antiques if they looked the part—regardless of age. Since many objects, such as baskets, woodenware, and pottery, are hard to date precisely, this solution pleased almost everyone.

As the 1960s dawned, a new situation developed. Victoriana became the rage, and because the Victorian era extended up to the time of the First World War, collectors who pursued this interest suddenly found themselves peering across the very narrow gap between Victoriana and the roaring twenties—and all that lay beyond. Tentatively, they began to collect Art Deco objects, adding them to their already acceptable accumulations of similar Victorian Art Nouveau accessories.

The forbidden wall was breached, and hordes of hungry collectors poured into the promised land of the 1920s and 1930s. For some it was a matter of nostalgia—they were collecting the very objects they had grown up with. For others it was more practical; Depression glass, Fiesta ware, and Jim Beam bottles were cheap and plentiful. It was possible to build a collection without mortgaging the homestead, a situation that even as early as the mid-1960s no longer existed in the world of classical antiques collecting.

The dealers responded to this new interest. A mass of Occupied Japan figurines, Orphan Annie premiums, and 1940s comic books began to appear on dealers' shelves and at shows. Some promoters responded negatively. Secure in the continuing boom for "true" antiques, they

Opposite: Wurlitzer jukebox; 1940–50; $3,500–4,500. *Left:* Whiskey and medicine bottles; late 19th–early 20th century; $3–15 each. *Below:* Antiques shop interior. The clutter is in the best Victorian tradition.

Below: Overstuffed sofa and two chairs in walnut veneer; 1935–40; $3,000–5,000 the set. Bar in walnut veneer; 1930–40; $750–1,000. *Below right:* Art Nouveau bronze table lamp with beaded-glass shade; 1910–20; $275–350. *Bottom:* Art Deco plaster and cardboard fireplace; 1930–40; $90–140. Set of rattan furniture; 1930–40; $900–1,150. *Opposite:* Dressing table and mirror in walnut veneer; 1938–45; $275–375.

shut the doors on the new dealers and their merchandise. But other show managers embraced the new objects, and the public swarmed to buy. The collectibles boom was on!

Collectibles can be defined as objects less than a hundred years old, but as a matter of practice the term is almost always confined to pieces manufactured since 1920. Moreover, at most collectibles shows it is evident that most of the merchandise displayed dates from the 1930s, 1940s, and even the 1950s. It is also clear that although collectibles are very much American in the sense that they are collected here by Americans, many of them are of foreign origin. In the international world in which we live, national boundaries have less and less to do with collecting. Much art glass, for example, was made outside the United States—as, of course, were all Occupied Japan ceramics. Yet no book on American collectibles would be complete without these foreign-made items.

The present-day collector will observe that, unlike during those halcyon days of the 1960s and early 1970s, some collectibles are no longer inexpensive. Oak furniture made by Gustav Stickley in the early 1900s has sold for as much as $14,000 for a single desk and chair. Certain pieces of 1920s carnival glass command prices in the thousands, and the same is true for rare commemorative or special-issue Jim Beam whiskey bottles, though the latter date only to the 1960s. But it is still possible to purchase interesting things for reasonable sums—it just requires patience and knowledge. The patience is an acquired talent—it is our hope that the chapters of this book will provide the knowledge. However, one

Opposite top: Vase; by Van Briggle Art Pottery; Boulder, Colo.; 1920–30; $110–130. *Opposite bottom:* 1900s-style office with oak furniture. Flat-top desk; $425–475. Library table; $325–350. Swivel chair; $145–170. Combination chair and coat hanger; $75–90. *Left:* Oak dining table; 1905–15; $2,000–2,500. Set of four oak "V-back" side chairs; 1905–10; $1,750–2,000. Brass chandelier; 1900–10; $4,500–5,000. An extremely rare piece. Hammered-copper serving plate; 1910–12; $650–700. All pieces by Gustav Stickley.

13

should also be aware of some of the unusual factors that are affecting today's market.

In the first place, inflation and the steady decline in the purchasing power of the dollar have led to a situation in which many people feel that objects are worth more than money, particularly if the money can be put into objects that will increase in value over a period of time. Thus, for the first time, speculation has entered the collecting field. People with little knowledge of or real interest in either antiques or collectibles have decided to put their wealth into these objects rather than into stocks or bonds. This is unfortunate for the true collector and appreciator of these objects because it means that at best he will have to pay more for his acquisitions and at worst he will not be able to afford them at all. Longing for the "good old days" will not take the speculators out of the market. Moreover, some wise collectors who purchased things they loved in the 1950s and 1960s are discovering to their delight that these objects have increased in value tenfold or more. Only the most obtuse collector will ignore the investment potential in his acquisitions.

Another factor the collector must consider is the auction phenomenon. Before the Second World War, with the exception of a few auction houses in major cities, auctions served primarily to redistribute used household goods and farm equipment. With the antiques boom, dealers and collectors discovered that there was gold in those old houses and barns, leading to an unparalleled growth in the auction business.

In the 1970s, auctions have become a way of life for many collectors. Oper-

Opposite: Dressing table, stool, and mirror in maple veneer; 1930–40; $285–435 the set. Clock; 1920–40; $65–90. Wall light sconces; 1935–45; $75–115 each. Feather hats; 1930–40; $20–35 each. Mannequin; 1925–35; $85–145. *Above:* Morris chair in oak and leather; 1901–16; $2,500–3,200. Footstool in oak and leather; ca. 1912; $650–800. Music cabinet in oak; 1910–12; $3,000–4,200. All pieces by Gustav Stickley.

ating on the sometimes erroneous theory that they can always buy cheaper at an auction, collectors have swarmed to the auction galleries. The auctioneer has the problem of providing merchandise. This competition for salable goods—be they early paintings or the art pottery of the 1900s—explains the recent change major auction galleries have made in the percentage fees that they charge for their services.

American auctioneers have traditionally charged a percentage of the amount realized at a sale to cover their services in promoting and selling the goods. This charge has generally ranged from 15 to 25 percent and is payable by the consign-or whose merchandise was sold. However, the recent trend is to charge the consignor less (usually 10 percent)—thus encouraging consignments—and to pass the cost on to the purchaser in the form of a 10 percent premium added to his purchase price. Collectors have been unhappy with this innovation, but it has had no appreciable effect on buying or attendance at auctions. Nevertheless, collectors attending auctions should keep in mind that they will often have to pay their bid price plus 10 percent.

Unfortunately, collectibles enthusiasts must now also contend with dishonesty. High prices and the possibility of making substantial profits bring out the

Above: Oak table; $4,000–5,500. Glass-fronted china cabinet in oak; $1,900–2,700. Oak bench; $1,800–2,700. Fall-front desk in oak; $4,200–5,000. Hammered-copper chafing dish; $800–950. All pieces by Gustav Stickley; 1903–17.

Opposite: Extension table in oak; 1910–25; $375–475. Set of six press-back chairs in oak; 1890–1900; $450–600. Apothecary shelves in oak; 1880–1900; $2,500–3,200.

Display of advertising items set up in a simulated country store.

Top: Fiesta ware; 1935–45; $3–25 each. Round pedestal-style dining table in oak; 1920–25; $450–550. Set of six oak side chairs; $395–500. *Above:* Utilitarian glass from various manufacturers; 1930–40; $3–30 each. *Right:* Nippon Japanese porcelain tea set in American-made chrome frame; 1920–30; $140–215.

worst in some people. Reproductions of collectibles are becoming all too common. They range from increasing the value of an Austrian Lotz vase tenfold by inscribing on it a bogus Tiffany signature to the wholesale reproduction of various popular pressed-glass patterns. The best defense against this sort of chicanery is knowledge. The more you know about your chosen field, the less likely you are to be fooled. Lacking this knowledge, the would-be collector is advised to buy only from knowledgeable dealers who are willing to guarantee their merchandise. Anyone purchasing a piece that is worth a substantial sum is entitled to a written statement of authenticity signed by the dealer. If the dealer is unwilling to give such a statement, there may be a very good reason!

But disagreeable factors such as high prices and fakery are only a small part of the collectibles scene. For the most part, collectibles are alive and well, and this is due in no small part to their great variety. During the nineteenth century, the typical home was furnished with a surprisingly small amount of useful objects; and these were made from relatively few materials: glass, pottery, metal, wood, and textiles. By the end of the 1800s, however, the number of objects had begun to expand, and in this century expansion has become deluge. Not only did people become better off financially during the past seventy years (and therefore better able to afford the things that we now regard as collectibles)—there was also a great increase in the number of materials from which these objects could be made.

Early in the century celluloid appeared as a medium for the manufacture of everything from dolls to imitation

Top: Woven-grass Indian basket; Southwest; 1920–25; $185–265. *Above:* Sterling silver coffee set; by Tiffany; 1890–1900; $2,500–3,200.

ivory. Celluloid was soon followed by Bakelite, which largely replaced wood in handles and tops, and finally came the plastics that today threaten to usurp the roles of all other materials. Plastics of the 1950s and 1960s are already becoming valued collector's items.

New metals have also entered the field. To the pewter, tin, and iron common in the 1880s have been added aluminum, stainless steel, and chrome. Chrome, in particular, is the metal of the 1920s and 1930s. Chrome's shining, readily cleaned surface was particularly suitable for use on the modernistic tables and in the sleek furnishings of the period.

Pottery and glass, of course, are not new to us, but the roles they have played in the past century are quite different from their traditional ones. The rise in the 1880s of the small potteries and glassworks devoted to making art glass and art pottery led to the development of a whole new area of collectibles. Names such as Galle, Rookwood, Tiffany, and Weller guarantee lovely objects, all of them collectible, but few of them now inexpensive. For bargains, the collector

Left: Pair of Art Deco tubular-steel sofas 1938–40; $6,500–9,500. These sofas are similar to prototypes by the designer Courvoiser. *Above:* Settle bench in oak; ca. 1901; $5,000–8500. Room divider of oak; ca. 1912;

$5,200–6,500. Library table; ca. 1901;
$2,100–2800. All pieces by Gustav Stickley.
Slag glass and bronze lamp; by Louis
Comfort Tiffany; 1910–15; $6,500–8,500.

23

Right: Mission-style sideboard in oak; 1910–20; $450–700. *Opposite:* Art Deco table and chairs; by Alvar Aalto; 1935–40; $3,500–5,500. Cabinet in blond maple and mahogany; 1935–40; $750–1,000. Mirrored glass panel; 1930–40; $3,500–5,500. Fiesta ware salt and pepper shakers; 1935–45; $6–18 each.

Below: Bureau doll; 1925–35; $35–55. Bedside table in painted pine; 1935–40; $125–145. *Right:* Advertising poster in cardboard, paper, and tin; 1890–1920; $165–550 each.

must look elsewhere.

Well-made factory furniture in the sleek, blond style of the Art Deco period is still available at reasonable prices. Much the same may be said of wicker furniture. It is possible to furnish a whole house in 1920s wicker at prices far less than one would pay for comparable contemporary furniture.

There are also bargains in glass. Much 1930s glass is still underpriced, and with the exception of certain hard-to-find colors and patterns, the ever-popular Depression glass is still available and inexpensive. A similar situation exists in the field of pottery. Fiesta ware is still readily obtainable, and the less-well-known variants, such as Harlequin and Luray, represent real bargains.

For those who prefer textiles, clothing of the 1920s and 1930s is still showing up in thrift shops and at house sales at unbelievably low prices. Although the same may not be said for the extremely popular Victorian garments, Victorian jewelry, if not set with precious stones, can be a fine investment. Also available are later pieces, particularly costume jewelry.

Quite simply, the world of collectibles is full of real bargains—and not all of them have been discovered yet. A crafty collector, wanting to get a little jump on the competition, might just thumb through a couple of those reprints of early-twentieth-century Sears Roebuck and Montgomery Ward catalogs. They tell us what was available back then, and you will be surprised at just how much is still waiting to be discovered.

Opposite: Piano in tiger wood; 1929–31; $1,400–1,900. Pair of stools in laminated wood; 1930–40; $350–500. Glass wall plaque; by Lee Lowery; 1930–35; $2,500–3,700. Art Deco scatter rug; 1930–40; $75–95. *Above:* China cabinet in oak; 1910–25; $400–485. Art pottery, by Artus Van Briggle; $50–900 each.

INTRODUCTION TO THE REVISED EDITION

The first edition of this book appeared in 1979 amidst a tremendous boom in collectibles. Everything from Tiffany glass to Jim Beam bottles was in demand, and prices were rising on an almost daily basis. However, within a few months recession set in, and the resultant decline in the economy severely affected the collectibles market. Today, however, the turnaround of '82 continues into 1983; and most collectibles are once more viable investments.

However, as in the world of earlier antiques; certain patterns have emerged. Good things bring good prices. The best things bring the best prices. Top items such as Tiffany, hard to find art pottery, Stickley oak and desirable American Indian basketry, were scarcely affected by the recession. Those who collected them continued to buy, and with the entry of more buyers into the market prices have soared. On the other hand, depression glass, machine made bottles, Fiesta ware and other low priced objects declined in value bcause those who collected them were hardest hit by the recession.

Even today prices in these and related areas are climbing slowly if at all.

Also, faddish items such as horn furniture and old clothing have not done well; while solid and traditional areas like bronzes, sterling silver, jewelry and good quality Art Nouveau and Art Deco accessories have weathered the storm and are climbing to new heights. Other areas that look particularly promising now are art glass, clocks and watches and radios; especially the plastic Art Deco models of the 1930s which have undergone remarkable price increases in the past year.

Unexpected rises and declines in prices are more likely to occur in the field of newer collectibles, and part of the price that one pays for adventuring into such areas as Japanese robot toys of the 1950s and paper memorabilia (be it Beatle or Super Bowl) is uncertainty. However, the collectibles collector tends to be younger, bolder and more of a chance taker than those who seek out traditional antiques; so he or she is often willing to take the risk in order to have the fun, excitement and sometimes the profit of breaking new ground. And, for those who crave this sort of excitement, now is the time!

Overstuffed couch. 1930–40; $600–800. Coffee table in maple veneer; 1935–45; $80–120. Occupied Japan tea set; 1945–52; $65–95. Occupied Japan vase; 1945–52; $20–30. Lamps; 1935–40; $80–115 the pair. *Opposite:* Dentist's cabinet in mahogany; 1910–15; $1,250–1,750.

Furniture

People who collect American furniture manufactured during the past century are presented with a bewildering variety from which to choose. They are confronted with furniture styles that range from the myriad styles of the Victorian period to the "Danish modern" that is still popular in many contemporary homes. They encounter a great deal of factory-made furniture as well as a great deal of furniture that was made—wholly or in considerable part—by hand. They are overwhelmed with golden oak, but soon discover that there is abundant furniture available made from other woods, such as pine, mahogany, rosewood, and walnut. They also find furniture made from other materials, such as plywood and tubular steel. It is a field of infinite variety and opportunity.

To start at the beginning, we must turn to the furnishings of the late nineteenth century. By the time of the 1876 centennial, American furniture was so different—in both design and method of construction—from the furniture that had preceded it that the public could easily accept the earlier pieces, which included Federal- and Chippendale-style furniture, as mementos of an almost forgotten past. And this was the furniture that their grandparents had used—and in some cases were still using! To understand how so great a change could come about in so short a period of time, one needs to know something of the factory system and its development in the United States.

Until about 1840, most American furniture was made by hand: it was put together by craftsmen who through long apprenticeship had learned how to make a piece from start to finish, from planing down the rough wood to applying the final paint or varnish. During the late Empire period—a period of massive and somewhat overdone furniture—small furniture-making factories began to appear, and the men who worked in these small factories had rather specialized duties. One would turn legs on a lathe, another would carve moldings, yet another would paint. Pieces would thus be put together not by a single cabinetmaker but through the joint efforts of several workers.

The exigencies of the Civil War greatly accelerated the process of job diversification. In support of the war effort, great factories sprang up throughout the northern United States, and the first production lines made their appearance, with each employee performing only a small part of the total task. After the war, as the territories were opened to settlement, the pioneers moving west needed large quantities of furniture. In the past, such needs had been filled by small shops located in the developing areas, but the new methods of construction had changed all that. Huge furniture factories were built in Grand Rapids, Michigan, and other midwestern cities, and thousands of pieces of inexpensive, machine-cut and production-line-assembled furniture poured out to fill the need. Quickly made and inexpensively sold, much of this furniture was not well constructed, and "Grand Rapids" became a synonym for cheap and shoddy.

However, it is possible that those early critics—many of whom were still accustomed to hand-crafted furnishings—judged too harshly. Today's collectors have discovered that late-nineteenth-century furniture was, for the most part, better made than the furniture that we have available today. Moreover, the nineteenth-century householder was offered a remarkable variety of furnishings. The Victorian era was eclectic: rather than adhering to a single clearly defined style, such as Queen Anne or Empire, designers used elements of many different styles in combination. Names such as Renaissance Revival, Gothic, and Egyptian Revival were used in an effort to create the illusion of unifying styles, but such really did not exist. Most pieces of Victorian furniture show the influence of several earlier styles. Sometimes, though not always, the result is pleasing.

Inevitably, there was a reaction to such overelaboration. By the end of the century, one form and one wood came to predominate. In England,

Art Deco dining room table and set of six chairs in laminated walnut; 1930–40; $5,000–7,000 the set.

as early as the 1860s, the poet and designer William Morris (1834 to 1896) preached the virtues of simple oak furniture designed on the order of ancient Gothic pieces—with the joinings and construction clearly exposed (something the Victorian cabinetmakers had always tried to avoid). But Morris was before his time, and it was not until the 1880s that the public came to accept his ideas. The result was a type of plain, rectilinear furniture that is often called Mission Oak because of a fancied resemblance to the furnishings made in the early Spanish missions of the American West.

From the 1880s on into the 1920s and even 1930s, vast quantities of oak household and office furniture were manufactured throughout the United States. Some of this was in the Mission style, and some was in the so-called Eastlake style, a slightly more decorative and curvilinear mode patterned on the designs of Charles Lock Eastlake (1836 to 1906), whose book *Hints on Household Taste* had a great influence on many American homemakers.

However, the greatest American exponent of oak furniture was Gustav Stickley (1857 to 1942). Born on a midwestern farm, Stickley was trained as a chairmaker and later established a furniture factory in Syracuse, New York. The lines of his furniture, which was almost totally without decoration, were extremely severe. Moreover, his furniture violated Victorian tenets in an even more fundamental way—it was almost entirely handmade!

Though they displayed some elements of the Mission style as well as certain features found in American colonial furniture, Stickley's pieces were distinctly his own. Angular and solid, made from oak, beech, or elm, they, in Stickley's words, had "strong, straight lines and plain surfaces to . . . emphasize the natural character that belonged to the growing tree."

From 1901 until 1916 Stickley produced chairs, tables, and case furniture, such as desks and chests of drawers, intended for sale to families of modest means. Most of these pieces were originally marked or labeled. He also designed simple, functional homes in which his furnishings might be used to greatest advantage. Unfortunately, Gustav Stickley's furniture was both too plain and too popular. It was easy to copy, and as soon as it began to sell well, a slew of cabinetmakers, including the Roycrofters of East Aurora, New York, and Stickley's own brothers, began to turn out very similar furnishings. As a consequence, the collector will frequently encounter pieces that look like Stickley but are unmarked or bear some variation of marks such as Cottage, Quaint, Art Craft, Mission, or Craft. None were made by Stickley's shop, but all are now quite collectible.

This competition combined with his own somewhat grandiose schemes (including a magazine-publishing venture and a gargantuan showroom in New York City) led to Stickley's downfall. He went bankrupt in 1915 and died alone and unheralded.

Nor did death put an end to the cruel tricks played by fate on Gustav Stickley. For, today, after being neglected for decades, Stickley furniture is once more the rage. But it is doubtful that the artisans and factory workers for whom it was designed will be able to afford it, for even the smallest and most ordinary examples sell for many hundreds of dollars.

Not all late-nineteenth- and early-twentieth-century furniture makers were as practical and aesthetic as the producers of Mission-style furnishings. The Victorian fondness for the gaudy died hard, and, in some ways, the last years of its existence were its most extreme.

Horn furniture is a good example. The 1880s and 1890s were great years for the sportsman. Buffalo hunters scoured the western plains. Elk, deer, and moose hunters decimated the herds. All these beasts had horns, and in the last decades of the century, furniture makers such as Charles Fletcher decided to make use of them. They made horn chairs (often with woven rawhide seats), desks, tables, hat and coat racks, even horn chandeliers. The horn of the longhorn cow was the one most frequently employed, though it was often combined with other types.

Originally used primarily in hunting lodges, country homes, and men's clubs, today horn furniture is considered a suitable embellishment to the dining or living room. It is not too common, however, and prices for the larger pieces have been growing steadily.

Horn was not the only unusual material used. Hunting lodges were also frequently furnished with rustic furniture made from branches and twigs of trees nailed or bound together without removing the bark. These rather crude pieces were known in upper New York State as Adirondack furniture, but similar examples (some with painted decoration) were made from 1890 until well into the 1930s throughout the forested areas of the northern United States. Though tables and chairs are most common, large wardrobes, chests of drawers, and even desks are known.

Rustic furniture, too, has undergone a revival. Not only are older specimens being collected and refurbished, but new pieces are being made. Newer examples can be distinguished from the originals by the lack of wear and aging in the wood.

Another form of rustic furniture was made of iron, cast and bolted together. Appropriately enough, the iron was often cast to resemble the rough surface of tree bark. Such furnishings were primarily a product of the late nineteenth century, and most were intended for use in the garden or on the sun porch. Chairs and settees are most common, though a few small tables can be found. Weight greatly limited the size and variety of this furniture.

On a more sophisticated level is the work of Michael Thonet (1796 to 1871) and his successors. Thonet, an Austrian, designed a variety of furnishings made from hardwood rods shaped under pressure. His pieces, which have a distinctly modern look, have long been called bentwood. Though other pieces were made, the technique lends itself particularly well to the forming of tables and chairs, including rockers. The flowing lines of these pieces owe much to the Art Nouveau style prevalent when Thonet was active.

Thonet's business prospered to such an extent that he opened overseas offices and shipped his furniture (which could be disassembled for transportation) throughout the world. Following expiration of the original design patent, bentwood was made by many different manufacturers, but for collectors the most desired examples are those bearing the mark of Michael Thonet.

Wicker is another furniture type that has persisted into the modern era. Made of wicker or rattan cane woven over a framework of wood or, later, bamboo, such furnishings were originally intended for use on the lawn or porch, but by the 1920s they had become popular living room and dining room furniture as well. Chairs, small tables, and sofas are the most frequently found examples, but cradles, planters, bookshelves, bedsteads, and desks are also available.

Although it looks fragile, wicker is strong, pliable, and quite weather resistant. Victorian examples can be distinguished by the narrower wicker employed as well as by the elaborate, curvilinear patterns in which they were woven. Post-1900 pieces tend to be loosely woven, of larger-diameter cane, and square or rectangular in form.

Wicker was at first made entirely by hand, but by the 1890s a certain amount of machine production had been introduced and today wicker furniture is handcrafted only in Asia and Africa. With the introduction of machinery came a simplification in style, so most collectors tend to favor the more elaborate Victorian examples. Recently, though, there has been an increase in interest in 1920s and 1930s wicker as collectors and homemakers discover that it provides a relatively inexpensive and extremely attractive form of furniture.

The early decades of this century brought no fundamental changes in furniture design. The Victorian mode prevailed, and Mission made its modifications, but nothing really new happened until the First World War. When the soldiers returned home after that cataclysmic engagement, they found a truly industrial society awaiting them. Just as after the Civil War, great technological advances had taken place during the war. And for this new society, only industrial design would suffice.

What that meant in the world of furniture soon became evident. Because machine production requires simple forms, furnishings in the 1920s became abstract in design rather than being based on natural forms. Decoration, too—where it existed—was simplified. The major sources of inspiration became the arts, where cubism prevailed, and the crafts, where the German Bauhaus school was preaching the doctrine of less is more.

Steel, the symbol of the new industrial age, played a major role. The Frenchman Marcel Bruer, inspired by the shape of bicycle handlebars, designed the first tubular steel chair, in 1925, and other designers, including the Finn Alvar Aalto, went on to combine the steel with shaped plywood and eventually to use the wood alone, creating flowing, curvilinear furniture.

Art Deco furnishings, whether of wood or metal, are characterized by rounded, industrial shapes and tooled steel accessories. But at the same time that forms were being simplified, modern technology made possible the use of extremely thin veneers, and a great deal of the furniture made during the 1920s and 1930s is finished in such veneers, particularly in the light blond woods so favored at the time.

Interestingly enough there was a countervailing movement. Many people were simply too conservative to accept the new mode. For them, American cabinetmakers offered a continuation of the mass-produced furniture of the early 1900s. This furniture was in the so-called Jacobean manner, with great knobby turnings, elaborate machine-cut moldings, and darkly stained woods. Such furnishings were sturdy—if boring—and like so much early-twentieth-century furniture, they have now been discovered by collectors.

Furniture of the past century offers an increasingly interesting field for the collector. Both in variety and availability it generally surpasses the furniture of earlier American periods. However, certain areas, such as Gustav Stickley furniture, are already overpriced, and the wise investor will buy now.

Oak occasional table with cabriole legs; 1920–25; $130–165.

Child's side chair in turned oak with laminated wood crest rail; 1915–25; $40–65.

Mission-style oak armchair; 1905–10; $850–1,100. The plain lines and exposed construction of this piece are in the best Mission style.

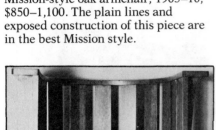

Oak collapsible rocker-stroller combination; 1900–10; $200–275. This chair reflects the Victorian fondness for furniture that served more than one purpose.

Oak rocker with cane seat and spindle back; 1890–1900; $135–175. The design on the crest of this chair was created by use of giant pressing machines—hence the name "press back."

Oak press-back rocker with well-turned spindles; 1900–10; $160–210.

Oak occasional table with curved cabriole legs and paw feet; 1890–1905; $200–275. An example of quality in acommon form of table.

Oak commode; ca. 1910; $145–185. ▶
Commodes of this sort were very
common in the early 1900s.

Oak library table with pedestal short-
ened to serve as a coffee table; 1915–
25; $300–375.
▼

Oak chest of drawers with
marble top and ceramic
inlay; 1910–20; $325–350.
This much decoration is
unusual with oak of this

Oak chest of drawers with
marble top and ceramic inlay;
1910–20; $300–375. This much
decoration is unusual with oak of
this period.

Oak ladies' dressing table; 1910–
20; $245–325. An unusually
small size.

Art Nouveau oak shaving stand; 1890–
1910; $400–500. Oak in the Art
Nouveau mode is relatively hard to
come by.

Oak file cabinet with writing surface top; 1920–30; $320-400. From 1890 until well into the 1930s, most office furniture was made of oak.

Interior of elaborate oak armoire; 1920–30; $900–1,200. Shows well-made drawers and shelves. This piece is nearly eight feet tall and seven feet wide.

Oak hanging wall cabinet; 1915–25; $130–180.

Oak double file box; 1930–40; $65–90

Oak dental cabinet; by Harvard Co.; Canton, Ohio; 1915–25; $1,400–1,800. Elaborate pieces of this sort are in great demand.

Oak desk and bookcase; 1890–1910; $800–$650–850.

Oak rolltop desk; by Standard Co.; 1910–20; $1,850–2,700.

Oak rolltop desk; 1910–20; $2,250–2,500. Oak office swivel chair; 1910–20; $115–130. Rolltop desks are bringing high prices today.

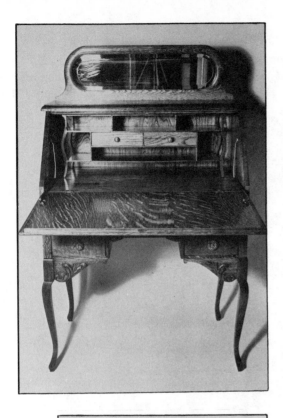

Oak fall-front desk with mirror; 1925–35; $350–500.
◀

Kerosene oil lamp with ceramic fount and glass shade; 1890–1900; $275–350.

Art Nouveau table lamp; 1890–1900; $750–900. This silver figure is an electrical work of art.

Copper and mica desk lamp; by Dirk Dirk Van Erp; San Francisco, Calif.; 1910–15; $1,800–2,100.

Bronzed pot-metal desk lamp with slag-glass shade; 1920–30; $150–200.

Turned wooden floor lamp with elaborate textile shade; 1925–35 $220–310. These were popular parlor and bedroom lamps.

Cast-iron floor lamp with green-glass inserts and textile shade; 1910–20; $175–235.

Pot-metal floor lamp in bronze finish with gold trim; 1920–25; $130–180.

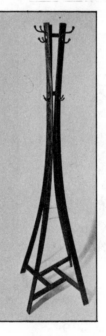

Turned oak coat rack; 1925–35; $65–85.

Mission-style oak coat rack; 1910–20; $85–115.

Oak pedestal-type plant stands; 1890–1910. *Left:* $175–215. *Right:* Mission style; $185–225.

Victorian Gothic oak umbrella stand; 1880–90; $80–120.

Oak revolving bookshelves; 1920–30; $175–225. These Mission-style shelves are relatively uncommon.

Oak and cast-iron combination mirror and coat rack; 1890–1900; $155–195.

Mission-style oak mirror; 1920–30; $75–115.

Left: Miniature oak extension table; 1910–20; $45–70. *Right:* Miniature oak bureau; 1890–1900; $60–90. Both pieces were intended to serve as toys or, possibly, as salesman's samples. ▶

Oak player piano; by Gulbransen-Dickinson Co.; New York, N.Y.; 1900–10; $4,500–5,500.

Miniature Empire-style pine fainting couch; 1880–90; $65–80.

Eastlake-style oak table; 1900–15; $225–275.

Miniature oak morris chair; 1920–30; $135–195. A salesman's sample in the Mission style. Eastlake-style oak table; 1900–15; $225–275.

Eastlake-style child's collapsible walnut rocker; 1880–90; $125–165.

Eastlake-style oak dining table; 1920–1930; $400-600. Dining tables remain the most popular of oak furniture.

Oak and leather footstool; by Gustav Stickley; 1905–12; $500–650. There are many oak footstools, but few bear the Stickley signature.

Oak and wicker desk lamp; by Gustav Stickley; ca. 1912; $1,750–2,250. The craze for signed Stickley pieces has inflated the price of this uncommon lamp.

Oak plant stand with tile insert top; by Grueby Faience Co,; 1901–02; $1,200–1,600. Designed by Gustav Stickley.

Miniature steerhorn armchair with felt upholstery; 1880–1900; $750–850. This rare example is possibly a salesman's sample.

Steerhorn platform rocker with upholstery; 1880–90; $1,200–1,650. Horn furniture is in great demand today among certain collectors.

Elk-horn and leather side chair; 1880–90; $900–1,100.

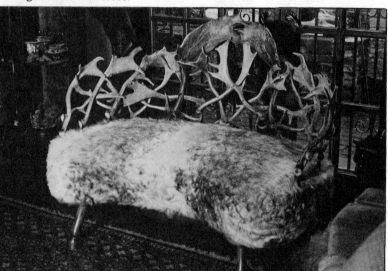

Moose-horn sofa; 1880–1900; $2,200–3,000. Sofas in horn are rare and desirable.

Elk-horn and wood desk; 1885–1900; '; $1,900–2,300.

Deer-horn and carved-wood magazine rack; 1900–10; $350–450.

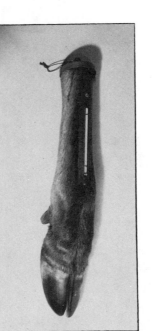

Thermometer mounted on the foot of an elk; 1915–25; $75–105. Grisly trophies of this sort were popular with early-20th-century sportsmen.

Wine cooler constructed from an elephant's foot mounted in wood and brass; 1900–10; $550–750.

Wooden hat rack or hall tree with two carved bears; 1900–10; $1,800–2,300.

Wooden umbrella rack; 1890–1900; ; $900–$750–950.

47

Library steps; 1910–20; $30–50.

Front: Wooden storage or trinket box decorated with small carved bear; 1910–20; $75–125. Rear: Wooden lamp decorated with small carved bears; 1910–20; $130–180.

Cast-iron fish tank; 1890–1900; $400–550. Cast-iron furnishings were extremely popular during the late Victorian period.

Stoneware garden armchair; 1880–85; $400–600. Made in the rustic form so favored by Victorians, cement and pottery garden chairs are relatively uncommon.

Bentwood chair for a child; 1920–30; $65–95. Developed by Michael Thonet, bentwood has proved so stylish and so practical that it is still in fashion.

Oak bentwood high chair with cane back and seat; 1910–20; $185–255.

Oak and ash bentwood platform rocker with cane seat and back; 1910–25; $250–350. A fine example of the bentwood form.

Bentwood child's rocker; 1915–25; $160–230.

Oak bentwood piano stool with cast-iron fittings; 1915–25; $65–95.

Natural finish wicker armchair with floral pillows; 1930–40; $175-225. This interesting piece has sockets in the arms for glasses and magazines.

White wicker rocker with floral material covering seat; 1920–30; ▲ $135–175.

White wicker pedestal table; 1930–40; $125–170.
◀

White wicker jardiniere, or planter, on stand; 1910–20; $75–120.
◀

Rattan and wood jardiniere; 1890–1900; $70–100.

Natural finish wicker double jardiniere; 1890–1900; $85–115.

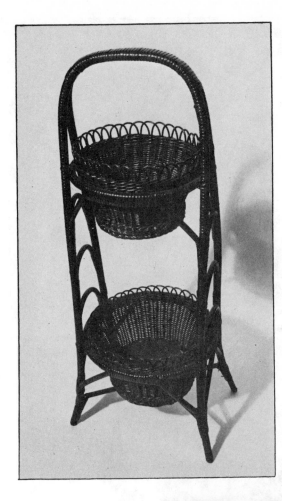

Rattan and sea grass occasional table; 1920–30; $80–110. The Art Deco form of this piece contrasts sharply with the material of which it is made.

Rattan and copper wastebasket; by Dirk Van Erp; San Francisco, Calif.; 1910—15; $650–850. Very few people can boast of a waste-basket made by a major American designer of the Arts and Crafts school.

Art Deco oak china cabinet; 1930–40; $250-340.

Overstuffed armchair in green baize; 1937–45; $300–425.

Art Deco overstuffed armchair in blue velour; 1930–40; $250–375.

Metal and Naugahyde armchair; 1930-1940; $225–275.

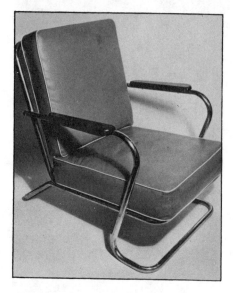

Walnut and Naugahyde side chair; 1930–40; $650–900.

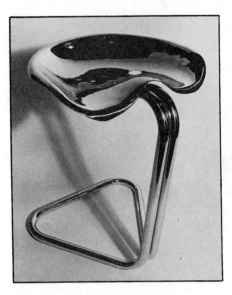

Art Deco mahogany side table; 1930–1940; $110–135.

Stainless-steel stool; 1950–60; $75–115.

Black lacquered end table; 1930–40; $85–135. *On table at left:* Glass and black enamel humidor and tray; 1930–40; $55–85. *On table at right:* Bronzed pot-metal desk lamp; 1930–40; $65–105.

Art Deco walnut veneer end table; 1930–40; $80–120.

Art Deco maple and walnut veneer dining table; 1925–35; $2,300–2,800.

White table with inset blue-glass top; 1935–45; $75–115. blue-glass tabletops were very popular during the late Art Deco period.

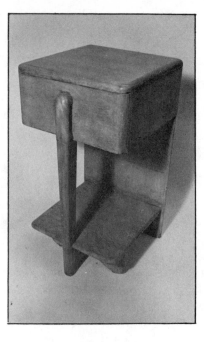

Art Deco maple veneer sewing table; 1935–45; $65-90.

Oak and oak veneer dressing table; 1935–45; $275–375.

Bleached mahogany veneer dressing table; 1935–45; $350-550. The "waterfall" style popular during the late Art Deco period.

Maple veneer kitchen cupboard; 1930–40; $300–425. These so-called Hoosier cupboards are popular in small city kitchens.

Walnut veneer, glass, and chrome ▲ bar; 1930–35; $1,000–1,500. Though in great demand, portable bars are rarely found intact.

Bird's-eye maple veneer bedside ▲ cupboard or nightstand; 1930–40; $100–150.

Art Deco inlaid maple drawers; 1925–35; $60–95.

Art Deco miniature maple veneer chest of drawers; 1930–40; $70–110.

Solid walnut desk; by Morris Adams, Ltd.; 1930–40; $900–1,200.

Oak and pine library shelves; 1925–35; $125–165.

◄

Bamboo bar counter; 1940–50; $300–450. Naugahyde and tubular-steel bar stools; 1940–50; $90–115 each. *On bar:* Set of cocktail shaker and glasses; 1940–50; $65–90.

Art Deco wood and metal standing floor ashtray; 1935–40; $75–95.

Painted pine standing floor ashtray; 1930–40; $75–115. Ashtray stands in the form of popular comic figures—such as Jiggs—were popular fixtures in many 1930s living rooms.

Sheet brass and black wood piano lamp; 1930–40; $165-235.

Sheet tin and steel ashtray, painted black; 1940–45; $30–45.

Glazed pottery and frosted glass table lamp; 1945–55; $46–65.

Emeralite desk lamp with green-glass shade and bronzed pot-metal base; 1910–20; $250–325. Mass produced for decades, Emeralite lamps are now once again in great demand.

Bronzed pot-metal desk lamp;
1935–45; $75–105.

Wooden figural table lamp; by
Rima; 1930–40; $200–285.

Tudor-style oak secretary desk with
leaded glass doors; 1910–30; $550–
600. A style popular with furniture
factories. ▶

Queen Anne-style oak dropleaf
table; 1920–35; $165–215. Furni-
ture factories often revived past
styles during the 1920s and
1930s.

Queen Anne-style oak and pine
tilt-top candlestand; 1920–30;
$85–135.

Tudor-style oak plant pedestal; 1930–40; $85–105.

Whatnot stand made of thread spools painted white; 1890–1900; $165–235. Making furniture from discarded spools was a popular Victorian pastime.

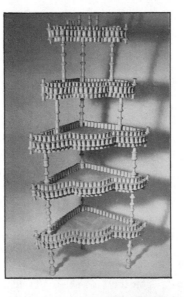

Sheet tin and steel radio speaker; 1925–30; $135–175. An unusual piece.

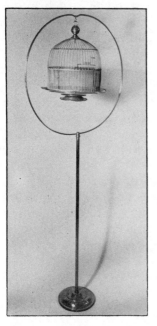

Brass birdcage; 1900–10; $175-235.

Jacobean-style oak ladies' dressing table with turned legs and brass fittings; 1930–35; $265–345.

Art Pottery

Collector interest in art pottery has grown steadily during the past decade, encompassing everything from the limited output of individual potters, such as George Ohr, to the essentially mass-produced wares of great factories, such as Roseville and McCoy. The spreading enthusiasm has brought not only sharp price increases but also a redefinition of art pottery itself.

The term *art pottery* originally referred to pieces produced in limited numbers by a relatively small group of studio potters. Most of their ware was wheel turned and hand decorated, and many pieces were signed—or at least initialed—by the artist. Typical of this period is the work of such renowned kilns as the Grueby Faience, the Cincinnati Art Pottery, and the Lonhuda Pottery.

Unlike the common household pottery of the period—which was generally produced in the most rapid way possible and had a minimum of decoration—art pottery was frequently quite elaborate. It was made from various clays, ranging from the common red variety used for bricks to fine white earthenwares and even porcelain. It was usually dipped in a glaze consisting of a mixture of ground glass or lead to produce a surface that, depending on the potter's intent, could be either shiny or dull, the latter being the so-called matte glaze.

Decoration could consist of the glaze alone—the color of which could be varied by the addition of different metallic compounds—or of designs either painted over the glaze (overglaze decoration) or on the piece prior to the final glazing (underglaze decoration). A good example of underglaze decoration is the brightly decorated white glazed ware known as majolica.

Other decorative devices include designs incised or impressed in the soft pottery prior to firing. Or the pot could have sections cut out of it to create an attractive design (reticulation). And, finally, smaller molded or hand-shaped pieces might be applied to the pottery to give it form and surface texture.

Unfortunately, even when managed by practical potters, early art potteries were frequently in financial trouble. Their wares were costly to produce, and only a limited number of consumers could appreciate or afford them. Only a relatively small amount of ware was produced, and much of it is now gone. Consequently, the small, pre-1900 potteries offer a limited opportunity for the average collector.

However, businessmen, such as Samuel Weller of Ohio, soon recognized the economic potential of art pottery and set about standardizing forms and creating "lines" characterized by a similar glaze and decoration. At first such pieces were individually shaped and decorated and were often artist signed, but it was not long before this approach was, in most cases, abandoned. Weller was the forerunner of such modern production potteries as Stangl, Hull, and Roseville (whose kilns turned out thousands of pieces in a single year).

As the number of art pottery enthusiasts has increased, new collectors have gravitated toward the less expensive and more readily available wares of these larger and often later potteries. The term *art pottery* has therefore come to include attractive tablewares and mass-produced vases and planters as well as the limited-edition studio work.

The range in style and decoration found in art pottery is truly remarkable. Some of the earliest artists, such as Thomas J. Wheatley and Matt Morgan, both of Cincinnati, adhered to the eclectic styles of the Victorian period, producing vases cluttered with applied flowers and Moorish ornamentation. Others working at the same time were strongly influenced by new artistic currents. Maria Longworth Nichols's famed Rookwood Pottery reflected its founder's appreciation of the oriental ceramics she had seen at the Philadelphia Centennial of 1876 both in its production of wares decorated in the Japanese manner and in the hiring of a Japanese designer, Kataro Shirayama-dani, in 1886.

Other studio potters, such as Teco Gates, were greatly affected by the teachings of the English artist and poet William Morris. Following Morris's admonition to avoid the often grotesque elaboration characteristic of Victorian decorative arts, they produced simple forms, often naturalistic in design.

The leaf, tree, and branch forms that Morris was so fond of were the hallmark of the Art Nouveau style, and few nineteenth- and early-twentieth-century art potteries were not affected by this mode. Perhaps the best application of Art Nouveau in American pottery was achieved by Artus Van Briggle, a young Colorado potter whose life was tragically cut short by tuberculosis. Recognizing that with Art Nouveau forms the least surface decoration is best, he developed a series of soft matte glazes that beautifully complemented the sinuous lines of his pottery. Other important kilns, such as Rookwood, Weller, and Roseville, produced art pottery in the Art Nouveau style.

As the twentieth century advanced, tastes changed. Increasing interest in the new forms of visual art, cubism, and the Italian futurist school began to have an effect on the plastic arts, too. The style known as Art Deco gradually came to dominate the output of many art potteries. One of the best-known producers of Art Deco ware is the Cowan Pottery of Liverpool, Ohio, but other shops, such as Coors of Colorado and Weller, also manufactured Art Deco ceramics.

The Great Depression signaled the end for most of the smaller and less efficient art potteries. With the buying public sharply diminished, only those factories that could produce a wide variety of inexpensive wares could hope to survive. The field of art pottery for the period 1930 to 1940 is therefore confined to the output of such factories as Weller and Roseville, the latter with one hundred and fifty different lines.

Following World War II, there was a revival of interest in art pottery, both in the collecting of older forms and the making of new. Influenced by Japanese and Scandanavian forms and methods, a new generation of potteries has taken to the field. Some of these potters have attained the status of factories, but most operate modestly, producing a few hundred or thousand pieces a year, most of which are offered for sale at craft fairs or through shops. It is this ware that is the true art pottery of today, and among these often struggling artists will be found the Van Briggles and the Ohrs of the second half of the twentieth century. Wise collectors are scouring the shops and fairs for the finer examples, and money is probably better spent on such ware than on the mass-produced commercial "art pottery."

If one wants to collect earlier examples, it is best to stick to marked examples from the more prestigious potteries. A collection of artist-signed pieces is always preferable, and these are almost certain to increase in value. As a practical matter, many collectors cannot afford such examples when available, but one should avoid those specimens that are neither marked nor identifiable from catalogs. Since so much art pottery was marked, unmarked pieces are less desirable.

Left: White vase with multicolored landscape set in electroplated silver base; ca. 1880; $825–950. *Center:* Green vase with yellow and white applied floral decoration; 1878–80; $600–750. *Right:* White vase with multicolored landscape; ca. 1800; $750–875. All by Odell & Booth Brothers Pottery; Tarrytown, N.Y. Odell & Booth operated less than five years, and its ware is extremely scarce.

Portrait tile in green glaze; by Low Art Tile Works; Chelsea, Mass.; ca. 1881; $735–865. This tile bears the initials of Arthur Osborne, who designed tiles for Low from 1877 until at least 1893.

Portrait tile in rich brown glaze; by Low Art Tile Works; Chelsea, Mass.; 1880–81; $600–750.

Blue vase with pink and green applied floral decoration; by Wheatley Pottery; Cincinnati, Ohio; 1880–83; $1,400–1,700. An early pottery, Wheatley's wares are rare and expensive.

Wall plaque in olive green glaze; by Chelsea Keramic Art Works; Chelsea, Mass.; ca. 1872; $2,000–2,750. This extremely rare stoneware wall piece was probably molded by Hugh Robertson, a member of the Chelsea firm.

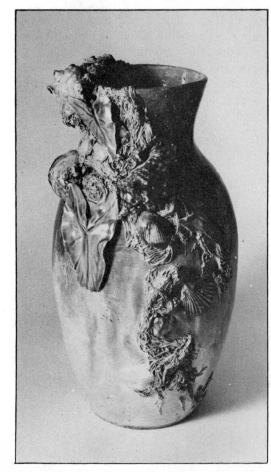

Double-handled bowl in blue glaze with gold overglaze; by Matt Morgan Pottery; Cincinnati, Ohio; 1883–84; $400–550. Morgan pottery was in operation only a year, and examples of its Moorish ceramics are rare.

Left: Handled vase in brown glaze; $700–850. *Center:* "Lolypop" vase in green glaze; $400–550. *Right:* Pilgrim flask in blue glaze with incised representation of a dog; $775–875. All by Chelsea Keramic Art Works; Chelsea, Mass.; 1875–89. ▼

Left: Vase in white stuccolike material with red and green applied floral decoration; ca. 1890; $750–875. *Right:* Cast mug in gray green glaze; 1887–90; $185-265. Both by Cincinnati Art Pottery; Cincinnati, Ohio.

Left: Blue porcelain box with pink and white applied floral decoration; $295–385. *Right:* Vase shaded light to dark blue with pink and white floral decoration; $800–1,000. Both by Faience Manufacturing Co.; Greenpoint, N.Y.; 1880-82.

Kerosene lamp base in pale tan glaze with gold highlights; by Avalon Faience Co,; Baltimore, Md.; ca. 1890; $875–1,075. Avalon was a division of Baltimore's Bennett Pottery.

Portrait tile of Gen. Ulysses S. Grant in green glaze; by American Encaustic Tiling Co.; Zanesville, Ohio; ca. 1885; $85–120. Portrait tiles were among the most popular of all art tiles.

Double inkwell in blue and tan crystalline glaze; by American Encaustic Tiling Co.; Zanesville, Ohio; 1880–90; $225–275. Though far better known for its tile, AETCO also produced a good line of pottery.

Left: Bowl; $195–245. *Right:* Vase; $215–285. Both by Lonhuda Pottery; Steubenville, Ohio; 1892–95. Both pieces are light brown with green and white floral decoration. This popular brown ground and underglaze decoration was developed by William Long, who later worked for both the Weller and Owens factories.

Left: Puzzle mug in rich brown glaze; ▲ 1888–1906; $225–275. *Right:* Drinking mug in clear glaze on red clay body made as a presentation piece; dated 1896; $385–425. Both by George Ohr; Biloxi, Miss. Partially because of its unusual form, partially because of its creator's eccentric personality, Ohr pottery has undergone a phenomenal increase in value during the last decade.

Left: Vase in green glaze. *Right:* Vase in tan glaze. Both by George Ohr; Biloxi, Miss.; ca. 1890; $375–475 each. Ohr pottery is characterized by extremely thin walls and distinctive glazes.

Left: Inkwell in the form of a ship's bell in yellow glaze on a brown base; ca. 1890; $475–600. *Right:* Miniature hat in blue glaze; ca. 1900; $275–400. Both by George Ohr; Biloxi, Miss.

Left: Rare unglazed white earthenware ▲ bowl banded in blue and pink; 1890–1900; $135–170. *Center:* Vase with crimped top in mustard and brown glaze; ca. 1900; $285–335. *Right:* Gourd-shaped bud vase in blue and green; ca. 1890; $235–275. All by George Ohr; Biloxi, Miss. Like much Ohr ware, these pieces are signed by the potter.

◀ *Left:* Footed bowl or planter in black glaze with blue and white Cyrano pattern; ca. 1898; $190–225. *Right:* Utopian-ware jug in glossy brown glaze with green and white underglaze floral decoration; ca. 1897; $230–275. Both by J. B. Owens Pottery; Zanesville, Ohio.

Plate depicting General Washington's headquarters at Newburg [*sic*], N.Y., blue on white; by Volkmar Pottery; Brooklyn, N.Y.; ca. 1895; $350–525.

Candlesticks in blue green glaze with gold highlights and bases; by Durant Pottery; Westchester County, N.Y.; early 20th century; $325–385.

Left: Small bud vase in green matte glaze; $135–185. *Right:* Vase in blue matte glaze; $365–445. Both by Grueby Faience Co.; Boston, Mass.; 1897–1910. During its relatively brief existence, this pottery produced high-quality matte-glazed ware in classic forms. ▼

Left: Footed bowl in pink glaze with ▲ blue interior. *Right:* Round vase in shades of pink. Both by Volkmar Pottery; Brooklyn, N.Y,; ca. 1905; $180–230 each.

Portrait tiles of George and Martha Washington; by Beaver Falls Art Tile Co.; Beaver Falls, Pa.; 1899–1927; $775–925 for both. These pink and tan examples are among the more sought after art tiles.

White porcelain bisque mug; by Clewell Ware; Canton, Ohio; ca. 1908; $120–160. Though Charles W. Clewell worked from 1902 to 1955, he made only a limited amount of pottery. His pieces were usually given a metallic bronze coating. This example, of the sort called a Holland Stein, was never glazed.

Mug in green matte glaze in the Arts and Craft mode; by Teco Pottery, Terra Cotta, Ill.; ca. 1909; $165–245. Leaves, flowers, and similar naturalistic motifs are common on ware from this pottery.

Left: Aurelian glaze pitcher in chocolate and white on light brown ground; ca. 1900; $250–310. *Center:* Indian-style bowl in tan and white matte glaze; ca. 1920; $80–105. *Right:* Chengtu pattern vase in orange red matte glaze; 1920–25; $85–115. All by Weller Pottery; Zanesville, Ohio.

LaSa Ware vases with metallic overglaze decoration in iridescent gold; by Weller Pottery; Zanesville, Ohio; 1920–25. *Left to right:* $205–245; $300–450; $215–265. This spectacular line of pottery was developed by John Lassell.

Dickinsware vase with incised figures of Mr. Dombey and his son filled in black and white on a tan ground; by Weller Pottery; Zanesville, Ohio; 1900–04; $525–650. Pieces bearing the likenesses of characters from the works of Charles Dickens are among the most popular of Weller creations.

Left: Creamer; $65–105. *Right:* Vase; $80–115. Both by Cowan Pottery; Lakewood, Rocky River, and Cleveland, Ohio; ca. 1917. Both pieces are in iridescent shades of pink, blue, and green.

Art tile. *Left:* Head of a warrior in ▶ green glaze; by Cambridge Art Tile Works; Cambridge, Mass.; 1887–1927; $80–115. *Center:* Head of Lincoln in blue and white; by Mosaic Tile Co.; Zanesville, Ohio; 1920–30; $55–75. *Right:* Angel in olive green; by Trent Tile Co.; Trenton, N.J.; ca. 1930; $75–95.

Left: Compote in red and green crystalline glaze with reticulated (cut out) base; $250–275. *Right:* Blue vase with green and white applied floral decoration; $95–110. Both by Fulper Pottery; Flemington, N.J.; ca. 1920. A former stoneware pottery, Fulper produced much art pottery between 1910 and 1935. ▼

Handled ewer in the so-called standard ▶ glaze, yellow on tan ground; by Rookwood Pottery; Cincinnati, Ohio; ca. 1889; $474–575.

Velum pattern vase decorated by the painter Leonore Asbury, tan and blue on white; by Rookwood Pottery; Cincinnati, Ohio; ca. 1905; $135–185.

Three-handled chalice in green matte glaze decorated with raised abstract representation of a crab; by Rookwood Pottery; Cincinnati, Ohio; early 20th century; $310–400.

Bowl in tan and green matte glaze; by Rookwood Pottery; Cincinnati, Ohio; dated 1910; $115–175. This bowl, though fourteen inches in diameter, was a standard production piece. ▼

Bookend in the form of a reclin- ▲ ing leopard, light brown; by Rookwood Pottery; Cincinnati, Ohio; ca. 1925; $75–125. Animal forms and decorative devices were popular at Rookwood.

Rook or crow, mottled brown glaze; by Rookwood Pottery; Cincinnati, Ohio; ca. 1926; $195–265. The rook was adopted as a symbol of the Rookwood Pottery because the kiln's founder, Maria Longworth Nichols, had grown up near rook-filled woods in England. ◄

Consol set consisting of center bowl and pair of candlesticks all on elephant bases, pink and pale green; by Rookwood Pottery; Cincinnati, Ohio; ▼ ca. 1929; $180–240.

Figure of a woman on a horse in the style of DiChirico, white glazed earthenware; by Rookwood Pottery; Cincinnati, Ohio; ca. 1930; $325–425.

Left: Large deep blue vase; ca. 1919; $90–125. *Center:* Green flower frog; 20th century; $15–25. *Right:* Pale blue commemorative vase; 1934; $90–125. Made for Cincinnati meeting of the National Conference of Catholic Charities. All by Rookwood Pottery; Cincinnati, Ohio.

Left: Ewer in butter-fat glaze; ca. 1946; $185–235. *Center rear:* Vase, green on cream butter-fat glaze; ca. 1944; $190-235. Center front: Bowl in green matte glaze; ca. 1914; $55–85. *Right:* Bud vase, blue on gray drip glaze; ca. 1916; $90–120. All by Rookwood Pottery; Cincinnati, Ohio. ▶

Statuette in blue green matte ▲ glaze; by Artus Van Briggle; Colorado Springs, Colo.; ca. 1930; $75–100. This piece, made to fit into a matching bud bowl, was pictured in 1930–40 catalogs, where it was called "The Lady of the Lake" and described as a masterpiece of design.

Left: Cock, jewel glaze on white ▲ ground; ca. 1946; $130–155. *Center:* Cockatoo in white butter-fat glaze; ca. 1943; $165–245. *Right:* Female figure in green butter-fat glaze; ca. 1945; $135–175. All by Rookwood Pottery; Cincinnati, Ohio.

◀
Left: Squat blue green vase; ca. 1930; $20–25. *Center:* Tall purple vase; ca. 1922; $30–40. *Right:* Blue green vase; 1922–29; $30–40. All by Artus Van Briggle; Colorado Springs, Colo. Van Briggle was particularly fond of flowing Art Nouveau forms.

Left: Tan and green vase; ca. 1910; $500–625. *Center:* Vase in black matte glaze; dated 1907; $700–875. *Right:* Squat vase in mustard glaze; dated 1903; $650–750. All by Artus Van Briggle; Colorado Springs, Colo. These are rare colors.

Turquoise bowl; by Artus Van Briggle; Colorado Springs, Colo.; ca. 1950; $55–75. The glaze employed was described in catalogs as "velvet embroidery" in clay.

Pair of double candleholders in blue matte glaze with violet highlights; by Artus Van Briggle; Colorado Springs, Colo.; 1945. $30–45. When new the pair sold for $6.75. ▶

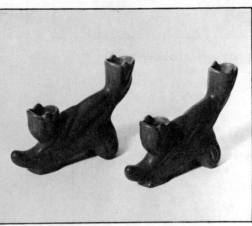

Vase, green and purple glaze in rich tones; by Artus Van Briggle; Colorado Springs, Colo.; ca. 1930; $65–90. Simple flowing forms and rich glazes ◀ characterize this ware.

Indian-head wall plaques marked "Big Buffalo" and Little Star," pink and peach; by Artus Van Briggle; Colorado Springs, Colo.; 1930–35; $175–245 the pair.

Bud vase in rose and green matte glaze; by Muncie Pottery; Muncie, Ind,; 1925–30; $35–55. Flowing glazes like this were typical of Muncie ware.

Pair of tall bud vases in rose and green matte glaze; by Muncie Pottery; Muncie, Ind.; 1925–30; $40–65. The Muncie Pottery was in operation from 1922 to 1939.

Left: $20–40. *Right:* Planter; $20–30. Both by Red Wing Art Pottery; Red Wing, Minn.; 1925–30. Both pieces are in green matte glaze on tan background with glossy green interiors.

Art Deco vase in pink glaze with green interior; by Coors Porcelain Works; Golden, Colo.; ca. 1930; $30–45. Though essentially utilitarian in nature, Coors pottery is often quite well formed.

Left: Teapot in the form of a chicken in yellow glaze; $20–30. *Right:* Pitcher in white glaze with brown highlights; $20–35. Both by Red Wing Art Pottery; Red Wing, Minn.; 1940s. These are the products of a stoneware factory turned to art pottery.

Teapot in tan and green glaze with ▶
yellow zephyr lily pattern; by
Roseville Pottery; Zanesville, Ohio; ca.
1947; $60–95. During its long life,
Roseville produced dozens of different
pattern lines.

Left: Apple blossom pattern wall ▼
pocket in blue with white floral
decoration; ca. 1948; $35–50. *Center:*
Snowberry pattern wall pocket with
green and white floral decoration; ca.
1947; $40–55. *Right:* Zephyr lily
pattern wall pocket in dark blue with
yellow floral decoration; ca. 1947;
$45–60. All by Roseville Pottery;
Zanesville, Ohio.

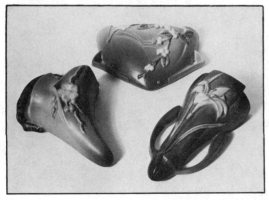

Left: Windsor pattern handled vase in ▲
blue glaze with green highlights; ca.
1931; $65–90. *Center:* Inkwell in
Rozane Egypto pattern in green matte
glaze; ca. 1906; $140–200. *Right:*
Egypto pattern footed bowl in green
matte glaze; ca. 1906; $165–235. All by
Roseville Pottery; Zanesville, Ohio.

◀ *Left:* Blue magnolia pattern basket-
handled vase with pink and white
floral decoration; 1943–44; $40–60.
Center: Peony pattern tray in pink and
green with yellow floral decoration;
ca. 1942; $45–65. *Right:* Water lily
pattern conch shell vase in green with
white floral decoration; ca. 1943; $25–
35. All by Roseville Pottery; Zanesville, Ohio.

Left: Pitcher in pink glaze with eagle
motif; $25–40. *Center:* Pink bud vase;
$10–15. *Right:* Blue vase; $15–25. All
by Niloak Pottery; Benton, Ark.; 1935–
40. All are in matte glazes.

Pair of vases in tan matte glaze; by Niloak Pottery; Benton, Ark.; ca. 1940; $15–30. Though better known for its marbleized wares, Niloak made much cast art pottery in solid colors.

Left: Two-handled bowl in red and green splotch glaze; ca. 1930; $25–40. *Center:* Three-handled sea green vase; ca. 1950; $15–25. *Right:* Olive green coffee warmer; ca. 1950; $10–20. All by Stangl Pottery; Flemington, N.J.

Ovenproof baking pot in the form of a nesting hen, brown glaze; by Hull Pottery Co.; Crooksville, Ohio; 1960–65; $25–40. Though some don't consider later Hull ware art pottery, many collectors collect it as such.

Multicolored plate in style of majolica; by Stangl Pottery; Flemington, N.J.; 1940–50; $20–30. Stangl is the successor to the old Fulper Pottery of New Jersey.

Left: One of a pair of saltshakers, green and yellow design on white; $8–15 the pair. *Center:* Pink teapot with green and white floral decoration; $25–32. *Right:* Planter in the form of a pig, pink and white; $12–18. All by Hull Pottery Co.; Crooksville, Ohio; ca. 1940.

Cookie jar in the form of Little Red Riding Hood, multicolored glaze on white ground; by Hull Pottery Co,; Crooksville, Ohio; ca. 1950; $50–65.

Cookie jar in the form of a bear, brown and red on white; by McCoy Pottery; Clarksburgh, W.Va.; 1943–45; $60–85. Like Hull, McCoy is a producer of the "new" art pottery.

Savings bank in the form of an eagle, brown and white; by McCoy Pottery; Clarksburgh, W.Va.; 1960–65; $10–15. Made for the Emigrant Industrial Savings Bank.

Wall plaque or Easter plate in white glaze; by Frankoma Pottery; 1972; $10–15. A modern art pottery, Frankoma's wares are attracting substantial collector attention.

Left: Sugar bowl; $10–15. *Center:* Wall pocket; $15–20. *Right:* Creamer; $15–25. All by Frankoma Pottery; 1960–70. All are in metallic green glaze.

Popular Pottery

At the end of the nineteenth century, the American pottery industry—until then a relatively coherent entity—split apart. The traditional craft potteries, unable to compete with the more efficient mass producers, failed and were replaced by the art potteries (discussed in the preceding chapter). These art potteries catered to a select few; their wares were expensive to produce and therefore cost more than the average buyer could afford. The rest of the industry, of course, was composed of the mass producers, the great factories of Ohio and New Jersey, which provided the bulk of the nation's essential ceramics.

This so-called popular pottery has recently drawn the attention of a growing number of collectors. It remains inexpensive, and it makes an excellent field for the beginning collector. Produced between 1900 and 1970—by such manufacturers as Homer Laughlin and Regal China—the field is comprised of ornamental figures, storage vessels, vases, and tablewares. Tablewares are probably the most open area today, and preeminent among tablewares is Fiesta.

In January 1936, the Homer Laughlin pottery company of Newell, West Virginia, introduced a spectacular line of dinnerware at the annual Pittsburgh Pottery and Glass Manufacturers' Show. Named Fiesta and designed by the English potter Frederick Rhead, the new ware combined modern design with strong color. Rejecting the traditional "busyness" of most prior tablewares, in which a great deal of floral decoration had usually been superimposed on a neutral background, the creators of the style opted for simple lines and bold, solid colors. The most sought-after colors are red and ivory, though cobalt blue remains a favorite of many collectors.

Fiesta, which once sold for a few pennies per piece, has been increasing in price, and collectors have begun to turn to other, similar ware. Chief among these is Harlequin, which was introduced by Homer Laughlin in 1938 and manufactured until 1964. Though made in many of the same colors as Fiesta, Harlequin was quite different in design. The bold lines and cone shapes of Harlequin were distinctly Art Deco in concept. The new line, moreover, was not marked, as Fiesta had been. Also, it was sold primarily through the Woolworth chain of dime stores.

Another popular tableware line of the 1930s and 1940s was Luray, which was produced by several manufacturers and came in a variety of pastel shades. Both Harlequin and Luray sell for substantially less than Fiesta, and it is possible to assemble complete dinner sets for modest sums.

Not all tableware of the period from 1930 to 1960 was inexpensive. Many potteries, both American and European, produced high-quality lines that were made in limited quantities and sold for substantial sums. Particularly where blessed with strong Art Deco design or decoration, European pottery by such makers as Carlton and Fraunfelter is fully as collectible as the homegrown product. In fact, with popular pottery—as with many areas of twentieth-century collectibles—the sophisticated enthusiast looks for the best, no matter where it may have been made.

Foreign-made pottery includes Occupied Japan collectibles. Japan has long been a major ceramics manufacturer. From the end of the Second World War until 1952, American military administrators controlled the Japanese potteries, and the ware was marked "Occupied Japan." These pieces, which range from fine china dinnerware to a multitude of pottery and porcelain figures in every imaginable style, were imported into this country in great quantity. Today, they rank as one of the major areas of American collectibles.

Perhaps the most appealing aspect of Occupied Japan ceramics is their variety. Some companies, such as Noritake and Satsuma, produced thin-walled, hand-painted porcelain in a tradition going back to the seventeenth century. Other factories turned out imitations of everything from Meissen china to contemporary Hummel figurines. The figural pieces are the most common.

There are hundreds of different examples, many of which can still be purchased for a few dollars each.

The United States was not devoid of figural pottery. Very little was made during the 1800s (the rare primitive examples in redware and the sophisticated china pieces from New York and Philadelphia are now both expensive), but by 1900 figurines in the Art Nouveau style had begun to appear. By the 1920s, these forms were abundant and had begun to assume the hard lines and sleek look of the Art Deco style.

During this period figural pottery was perceived primarily as a decorative accessory, something to go on a shelf or a table. It was never really collected for itself until the advent of the pictorial whiskey bottle in the early 1950s.

Throughout most of the nineteenth century, glassmakers produced figural whiskey bottles in various shapes and sizes. Their appearance was clearly intended to promote the sale of their contents, and it is doubtful that the manufacturers foresaw that the receptacles would be collected. Collected they were—to the extent that "historical flasks," as they are now known, may sell today for thousands of dollars each. For both technical and aesthetic reasons, though, very few similar ceramic vessels were produced.

In 1953, Kentucky's James B. Beam Distilling Company put on the market a pottery Christmas decanter (filled with bourbon whiskey, of course). This, the first of the so-called Beam bottles, was such a success that since then literally hundreds of similar containers have been manufactured by Beam and by such competitors as Ezra Brooks and Ballantine. Beam bottles were among the first of the "controlled collectibles"—the value of the item is directly related to the number issued and the decision as to quantity lies in the hands of the manufacturer.

While the collecting of figural whiskey bottles has expanded greatly over the past two decades, many collectors have completely overlooked the many interesting figurines of the 1920s and 1930s. One may find everything from saltcellars to bookends and powder jars. Both the mass-produced dime-store pieces and the sophisticated examples by fine potteries, such as Fulper of New Jersey, are available. Most pieces can be obtained inexpensively—it is just a matter of seeking them out.

Fiesta ware in cobalt blue glaze; 1936–39. *Left:* Covered casserole; $30–40. *Center top:* Coffeepot; $35–45. *Center bottom:* Sugar bowl with cover; $15–22. *Right:* Teapot; $30–42. Cobalt blue is one of the most popular Fiesta ware colors.

Fiesta ware in green glaze. *Left bottom:* Cream soup bowl; 1936–59; $15–22. *Left top:* Sugar bowl with cover; 1936–69; $10–17. *Right top:* Creamer; 1936–69; $7–14. *Right bottom:* Nappy; 1936–69; $7–10.

Fiesta ware in sky blue glaze. *Left:* Marmalade bowl; 1936–46; $40–55 (with cover). *Center:* Sauce boat; 1939–73; $15–20. *Right:* Salt and pepper shakers; 1936–73; $10–15 the pair. *Underneath:* Chop plate; 1936–59; $15–20.

Fiesta ware in ivory glaze. *Left top:* Deep dish; 1936–69; $10–15. *Left bottom:* Dinner plate; 1936–73; $7–12. *Right top:* Eggcup; 1936–58; $15–22. *Right bottom:* Ashtray; 1936–73; $15–25.

Fiesta ware in red glaze; 1936–43 and after 1959. *Left bottom:* Three-section plate; $10–15. *Left top:* Teacup and saucer; $15–24. *Right:* Demitasse cup and saucer; $30–40. Red is one of the least common and most sought after Fiesta colors.

Fiesta ware tidbit tray in yellow and sky blue glaze with stainless steel rod; 1939–69; $40–65.

Fiesta ware. *Left:* Mixing bowl in cobalt blue glaze; 1936–44; $15–22. *Center:* Bread and butter plate in rose glaze; 1936–73; $2–4. *Right:* Platter in turquoise glaze; 1939–69; $8–11.

Left top: Fiesta ware ice-water pitcher in yellow glaze; 1939–73; $20–25. *Left bottom:* Fiesta ware utility dish in yellow glaze; 1936–46; $10–17. *Right top:* Fiesta ware carafe in yellow glaze; 1936–46; $30–40. *Right bottom:* Harlequin ware sugar bowl with cover in yellow glaze; 1938–64; $8–14.

Harlequin ware in turquoise glaze; 1938–64. *Left:* Pitcher; $10–17. *Center:* Salt and pepper shakers; $4–7 the pair. *Right:* Teapot; $18–27. Somewhat softer colors and a distinctly Art Deco style set Harlequin off from the more expensive Fiesta.

Harlequin ware; 1938–64. *Left:* Platter in dusky rose glaze; $5–8. *Right:* Serving bowl in sky blue glaze; $6–10.

Harlequin ware; 1938–64. *Left:* Sauce boat in red glaze; $8–14. *Center:* Sugar bowl with cover in blue glaze; $9–17. *Right:* Nappy in red glaze. $6–11.

Harlequin ware in green glaze; 1938–64. *Left:* Water jug; $15–25. *Right:* Cup and saucer; $5–10.

Luray Pastels ware in pale green glaze; 1940–50. *Left:* Creamer; $3–5. *Center:* Sugar bowl with cover; $6–9. *Right:* Miniature pitcher; $6–10. Though not particularly popular in its day, Luray is fast becoming a new collector's favorite.

Harlequin ware; 1938–64. *Left:* Bread and butter plate in green glaze; $2–3. *Right:* Dinner plate in turquoise glaze; $4–6.

Luray Pastels ware in pale pink glaze; 1940–50. *Left:* Cup and saucer; $2–3. *Center:* Soup bowl $2–4. *Right:* Creamer; $3–5.

Luray Pastels ware in pale blue glaze; 1940–50. *Left:* Platter; $3–5. *Center:* Vegetable bowl; $3–4. *Right:* Sugar bowl with cover; $5–8.

Luray Pastels ware in pale yellow
glaze; 1940–50. *Left:* Dessert bowl; $2–
3. *Center:* Large platter; $5–9. *Right:*
Cup and saucer; $3–5.

Green ironstone teapot; by Hall
China Co.; 1938–50; $20–30.
This attractive ware was
designed for restaurant use.

Ovenproof syrup pitcher with
metal and plastic top, in white
glaze with red and green floral
decoration; 1945–55; $15–20.

Left: Red pottery storage vessel;
$35–45. *Right:* Blue water
cooler; $45–65. Both by Hall
China Co.; 1935–45. These pieces
were made for use in Westinghouse refrigerators.

Ovenproof water pitcher in
cream glaze with red, yellow,
and green floral decoration;
1945–55; $20–28.

Porcelain powder box with chrome wash; 1935–40; $20–35. Designed for use with Estee Lauder cosmetics.

Hand-painted porcelain plate; by ▲ Roycrafters; East Aurora, N.Y.; 1920–30; $50–75. This plate is typical of the fine artist-styled ceramics produced in limited numbers during this century.

Blue-on-white majolica serving plate; by Rambord; Pasadena, Calif.; 1930–40; $30–40. Ware of this sort was always sold in limited quantity.

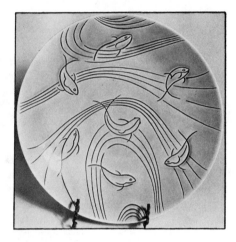

Rayalite Electric China Ware coffee urn, creamer, and sugar bowl with cover in cream glaze with green and orange decoration; by Fraunfelter China Co.; 1930–40; $500–600 the set. An extremely rare set.

Demitasse set in orange and black porcelain; by Carlton China Co.; 1930–40; $250–335.

Art Deco vase in cream glaze with pink and green decoration; 1925–32; $135–170.

Porcelain tobacco jar in pink and gold glaze; 1880–90; $250–300. The inscription indicates this piece was made as a gift.

Occupied Japan porcelain tea set in white with blue and pink flowers; 1945–52; $55–75. Made under the auspices of the American occupation forces, this ware has long been regarded as an American collectible.

Occupied Japan porcelain vase in pink and black; 1945–52; $25–40.

Occupied Japan chocolate set in cream and dark red; 1945–52; $75–115. Tea, coffee, and chocolate sets are among the most common Occupied Japan pottery.

Occupied Japan porcelain gravy boat in cream with green and yellow decoration; by Noritake China Co.; 1945–52; $45–65.

Occupied Japan majolica covered box in blue, green, and cream; 1945–52; $15–22.

Occupied Japan majolica toby pitchers in pink, blue, green, and tan; 1945–52. *Left:* $12–16. *Center:* $25–35. *Right:* $20–25.

Occupied Japan bisque Hummel-type figures; 1945–52. *Left:* Girl in yellow and green; $15–20. *Right:* Boy in green and blue; $20–25.

Occupied Japan bisque frogs; 1945–
52. *Left:* Green and blue; $7–12. *Center:*
Green and yellow; $15–20. *Right:*
Yellow, orange, and green; $7–10.

Pair of Occupied Japan bisque lamp
bases in shades of pink, gray, and
white; 1945–52; $45–70.

Jim Beam china figural whiskey
bottles. *Left:* Donkey clown; ca. 1968;
$15–25. *Right:* Donkey boxer; ca. 1964;
$20–30. A phenomenon of the 1950s
and 1960s, Jim Beam collecting
continues unabated.

Jim Beam china figural whiskey
bottle, Ponderosa Ranch; ca 1969; $15-
20.

Jim Beam china figural whiskey
bottle, Harolds Club; ca. 1968;
$10–15.

Jim Beam china figural whiskey
bottle, Beam's Trophy; ca. 1962;
$20–30.

Jim Beam china figural whiskey
bottle, Armanetti Liquors Award
Winner; 1969; $10–15.

Jim Beam china figural whiskey
bottle, New York World's Fair;
1965; $20–30.

Jim Beam china figural whiskey
bottle, Bing Crosby National Pro-
Am; 1970–73; $10–15.

Jim Beam china figural whiskey
bottles. *Left:* The Wonderful
World of Ohio; ca. 1966; $15–22.
Right: New Hampshire; ca. 1966;
$10–17.

Jim Beam china figural whiskey
bottles. *Left:* New Jersey; 1964;
$60–75. *Right:* Alaska Purchase
Centennial; 1967; $15–22.

Jim Beam china figural whiskey
bottle, 200th anniversary of the
California missions; 1967; $30–
40.

Jim Beam china figural bottles.
Left: Grecian flagon; 1965–70;
$15–20. *Right:* Florida seashell;
1968–69; $10–16.

White earthenware penny bank
hand painted in red and blue;
1910–20; $50–75. An example of
the country pottery still being
made in the United States during
the early 20th century.

Art Deco covered bowl in orange, green, blue, and black glaze; by Crown Devon Pottery; 1928–34; $65–80. A good example of the more spectacular commercial pottery of the 1920s and 1930s.

Pottery head with mask in pink, yellow, green, and blue; 1930–35; $40–60.

Art Deco pottery vase in black and white glaze; 1930–40; $35–45.

Three-piece bath salts containers in black and yellow glaze; 1932–38; $45–55.

Art Deco Phoenix ware vase in blue, tan, pink, and yellow glaze; 1925–35; $95–115.

Art Deco powder box in pink and blue glaze; by Fulper Pottery; 1930–37; $200–275.

Art Deco covered box in gray glaze with black speckles; 1930–40; $300–425. A rare and unusual example.

Pair of planters in crackled white glaze; 1935–40; $35–55.

Art Deco figure in white glaze;
1930–40; $35–55. In the style of
the cubists, this figure is a
popular 1930s form.

Ceramic elephant in white; 1925–35;
$75–110.

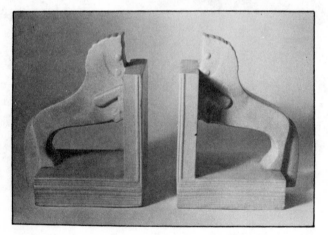

Pair of ceramic bookends in white;
1930–35; $60–85.

Pair of musicians in brown, black, and
white glaze; 1935–45; $55–75.

Miniature porcelain bathtub; 1940–45; $15–20. A novelty item probably intended as a trinket holder.

Ceramic zebra in black and white; 1933–38; $30–45.

Blue pottery inkwell in the form of an angel; 1905–15; $25–35.

Pottery shoe in brown glaze; 1900–10; $65–95. Intended for use as a whiskey sampler.

Art Glass

Art glass can be distinguished from its popular, or utilitarian, counterpart in much the same way that art pottery can be distinguished from common earthenware. In both cases the finer ware was made in limited quantities by sophisticated techniques and was sold for high prices to a discriminating and limited public. Unlike common glass, for which decoration was secondary to function, the main purpose of art glass was decoration, and each piece was viewed as a work of art.

Art glass has a long history—it was known in ancient Persia and in early Venice—but the flowering of the medium occurred in America and Europe during the late nineteenth and early twentieth centuries. Beginning about 1880, manufacturers such as Tiffany in the United States and Galle and Daum in France took advantage of technological innovations largely unknown to the ancients to create new colors and new methods of decoration that revolutionized the glassmaking industry.

The role that American manufacturers played in the development of art glass cannot be overestimated, and the greatest of the Yankee creators was Lewis Comfort Tiffany, son of the famous silver manufacturer. Tiffany trained as an artist and began working with glass in the 1880s. At first his interest lay mainly with stained glass, but by 1893, when he opened his own glassworks at Corona, New York, he had turned to art glass. In the following year he registered the mark *favrile* to cover his blown, iridescent glass, the weathered, multicolored surface of which reminded people of ancient glass. The brilliant shades of blue, green, brown, and yellow found in favrile, and the stylized motifs—likened to peacock feathers, seaweed, and fern fronds—were an instant sensation. Widely copied here and abroad, favrile was manufactured until Tiffany Studios shut down in 1920.

Favrile was not the extent of the Tiffany genius. Over the course of its existence the shop produced no less than five thousand different glass patterns, including many different types of vases and tablewares as well as the famous naturalistic lamps with leaded glass or blown shades, the latter frequently in the popular bell flower or lily patterns. The almost incredible prices now obtainable for some Tiffany pieces are proof of the skills of their creator. One should expect to pay substantial sums for much signed Tiffany. However, it is still possible to obtain smaller examples, such as stickpins and bowls, for prices in the low hundreds or even less. In fact, not all those stories about Tiffany shades purchased for pennies at flea markets are false. Unknowing people still let good pieces slip through.

One should not assume that Tiffany dominated the American art-glass market. He had worthy competitors. As early as 1874, the Mount Washington Glass Company of New Bedford, Massachusetts, was turning out large quantities of colored ware, including such specialties as amberina, a glass that was shaded from red to yellow, and the bluish white and pink ware called peach blow. Both types are very popular with today's collectors.

Another important New England firm was the Sandwich Glass Company, active at Sandwich, Massachusetts (1825 to 1888). The Sandwich works produced a substantial amount of art glass, including the lumpy, frosted ware known as overshot or craquele and the famous Mary Gregory enameled wares. Mary Gregory was a decorator who worked at Sandwich in the 1880s and specialized in quaint children's groups painted in white enamel on red, green, or blue glass. Her work is highly collectible today, though, unfortunately, its popularity has led to reproduction, both here and abroad.

The list of American manufacturers of art glass could go on and on, but it must include the brilliant cut and overlay glass made at the Pairpont Glass Company — a successor to Mount Washington — and the fine jadelike glass produced by the Steuben Glass Works of Corning, New York, during the directorship of the glassmaking genius Frederick Carder.

No true art-glass collector can confine himself to American products—not when the work of such greats as Galle and Daum is available. Emile Galle (1846 to 1894) was the outstanding French glassmaker of the nineteenth century. His experiments led to the creation of many unusual colors, including a vivid blue, but his basic interest lay not in color but in decoration. His shop, which remained active under other management until 1935, specialized in enameled glass as well as cameo. The latter was a form produced by cutting or etching through one layer of opaque glass to expose another contrasting layer that lay below it. Much Galle glass was made and signed, and much is available today, though prices for individual pieces are generally in the hundreds or even thousands of dollars.

Rivals of Galle were the Daum brothers, August and Antonin, also residents of the town of Nancy in France. Their acid-etched cameo glass, made after 1893, closely resembles that of Galle although it bears distinctive decorative motifs, such as bouquets of flowers, fruit, and pastoral landscapes. Daum ware is characteristically marked DAUM: NANCY.

A later glassmaker in the same community was Amalric Walter, who began working there in 1906, first using the Daum works, then, after the end of the First World War, acquiring his own shop. Walter specialized in pate de verre glass, which is created by allowing a mixture of crushed glass and metallic oxide colorants to harden in a mold.

In Austria the leading exponent of art glass was Max Ritter von Spaun, who took over the Lotz glassworks at Klostermühle in 1879. Obtaining the services of a disgruntled former Tiffany employee, Von Spaun was able, by the 1890s, to produce a good imitation of favrile ware. In fact, since much Lotz glass is unsigned, collectors have recently been plagued by Lotz pieces with bogus Tiffany signatures. However, Lotz ware, which was sometimes marked LOETZ-AUSTRIA for export, is a high-quality collectible in its own right.

Much art glass—as can be imagined from the dates of its manufacture—is in the Art Nouveau manner. However, after 1900 the flowing forms were gradually replaced by straight lines and geometric patterns ornamented only by black enamel on a clear or opalescent white glass. Cutting and etching became more pronounced in the 1920s, and those factories, such as Daum and Steuben, that continued into the Art Deco period modified their designs to appeal to the new taste.

While Art Deco glass cannot yet be said to rival in popularity the art glass made in the earlier era, there is little doubt that its day is coming. In fact, good-quality American and European art glass of the period from 1920 to 1945 represents an excellent investment, marked or not.

Stained-glass hot plate; by Louis Comfort Tiffany; Corona, N.Y.; 1885-90; $650–775. Tiffany experimented with stained glass before producing his famed iridescent glass.

Favrile; by Louis Comfort Tiffany; Corona, N.Y.; 1900–10. *Left:* Goblet; $250–325. *Right:* Pitcher; $350–425. Tiffany is best known for his iridescent favrile, which resembles ancient glass in color and texture.

Pair of favrile candlesticks; by Louis Comfort Tiffany; Corona, N.Y.; 1900–05; $450–575.

Favrile vase; by Louis Comfort Tiffany; Corona, N.Y.; 1898–1910; $550–600.

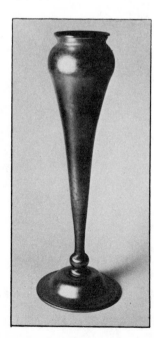

Favrile; by Louis Comfort Tiffany; Corona, N.Y.; 1900–15. *Left:* Plate; $300–390. *Right:* Bowl; $375–425.

Favrile scalloped bowl; by Louis
Comfort Tiffany; Corona, N.Y.;
1895–1905; $450–550.

Favrile bud bowl; by Louis
Comfort Tiffany; Corona, N.Y.;
1900–15; $700–900.

Iridescent glass lamp with
bronze base; attributed to Louis
Comfort Tiffany; Corona, N.Y.;
1895–1910; $1,500–2,200.

Seashell vase; by Steuben
Glass Works; Corning,
N.Y.; 1905–15; $350–425.
Under the direction of the
master glassmaker
Frederick Carder,
Steuben became one of
America's great art-glass
manufacturers.

Tiny aurene bud vase; by
Steuben Glass Works; Corning,
N.Y.; 1910–25; $175–225. This
white and gold vase is typical of
the pearllike finish known as
aurene.

Multicolored vase; by Quezal Art Glass and Decorating Co; Brooklyn, N.Y.; 1905–10; $250–325.

Violet vase encased in silver; by Quezal Art Glass and Decorating Co.; Brooklyn, N.Y.; 1901–12; $330–400. One of the smaller art-glass manufacturers, Quezal specialized in pieces encased in engraved silver.

Mercury glass; 1890–1900. *Left:* Goblet; $50–75. *Right:* Vase with multicolored enamel decoration; $75–110. Mercury glass, popular in the United States during the late 19th century, was made by injecting mercury between an inner and an outer wall of blown glass.

Blown glass footed compote edged in green; by Greystan Glass Co.; 1920–30; $150–225. An American company, Greystan was in business only a short time.

Agata glass miniature footed bowl; 1915–25; $60–65. Manufactured from a mixture of multicolored ground glass, agata was made at various American and European factories.

Mother-of-pearl pitcher; 1890–1900; $400–500. Also known as quilted satin glass, mother-of-pearl derives its distinctive pattern from air trapped between two layers of glass.

Mother-of-pearl vase in blue and white; 1890–1900; $250–350.

Mother-of-pearl oil lamps in pink; attributed to Sandwich Glass Co; Sandwich, Mass.; 1881–85; $275–325.

Mother-of-pearl glass; ca. 1890; *Left* and *right:* Pink salt and pepper shakers; $175–210 the pair. *Center:* Ping and white pitcher; $375–450.

Cranberry glass vase; 1890–1900; $70–90. Also known as ruby glass, cranberry's reddish color reflects the addition of gold oxide to the glass.

Cranberry glass bowl with clear
glass handles; attributed to
Sandwich Glass Co.; Sandwich,
Mass.; 1880–90; $100–125.

Cranberry glass hatpin holder
mounted in sterling silver; 1890–
1900; $50–70.

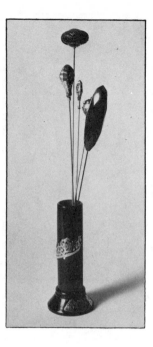

Pair of cranberry glass decanters
with etched designs in the
Bohemian manner; 1900–10;
$150–200. Because so much
colored glass was etched and cut
with floral and pastoral scenes at
the glass factories in central
European Bohemia, glass of this
sort is called Bohemian even
though much of it was made in
the United States.

Cranberry glass decorated in the
Bohemian manner; 1890–1910.
Left: Bowl; $90–110. *Right:*
Chalice; $65–90.

Stretch glass compote; by Mount
Washington Glass Works; New
Bedford, Mass.; 1885–95; $125–
155. The crackled surface of
stretch glass appeals to many
collectors.

Amberina glass pitcher; attributed to New England Glass Co.; 1885–1900; $315–385. Amberina glass shades from red to amber. It was developed in 1883 by Joseph Locke, a designer at New England Glass.

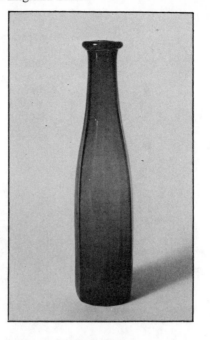

Amethyst glass perfume bottle; by Sandwich Glass Co.; Sandwich, Mass.; 1880–90; $75–100.

Iridescent green and yellow vase mounted in pewter; by Lotz (Loetz); Austria; 1890–1900; $325–425. The Lotz firm was Europe's answer to Tiffany, producing much fine favrilelike glass.

Overshot glass vase; attributed to Sandwich Glass Co.; Sandwich, Mass.; 1890–1900; $55–75. Overshot glass has an unusual frosted surface.

Left: Iridescent green bowl; $185–225. *Right:* Unusual aquamarine and brown vase; $550–700. Both by Lotz; Austria; 1890–1905.

Iridescent red vase mounted in pot metal; by Lotz; Austria; 1900–10; $235–285.

Green cameo glass bowl; by Emile Galle; Nancy, France; 1890–1904; $600–750. Cameo glass is produced by covering a piece of clear glass with a shell of colored glass and then cutting or etching away the colored glass to produce a contrasting composition.

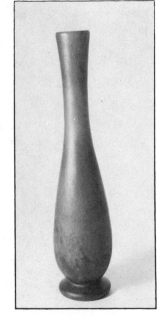

Green and gray cameo glass vase; by Emile Galle; Nancy, France; 1885–90; $1,200–1,900. The creator of modern cameo glass, Emile Galle is revered by art-glass enthusiasts, and his pieces are in great demand. This is an early example.

Cameo glass; 1895–1905. *Left:* Vase; by Emile Galle; Nancy, France; $700–850. *Right:* Vase; by August and Antonin Daum; Nancy, France; $400–500. Cameo glass by the Daum brothers is similar to that of Galle.

Cameo glass vase; by Daum; Nancy, France; 1900–20; $300–375.

Purple cameo glass table lamp; by Daum; Nancy, France; 1910–20; $1,600–2,100. Cameo lamps are hard to come by.

Multicolored cameo glass vase; by Muller Brothers; 1900–10; $950–1,050. Great detail makes this an important piece.

Cameo glass cologne bottle with sterling silver top; attributed to Stevens & Williams; England; 1890–1910; $400–525. In white and yellow, this piece is typical of the more classical English cameo.

English cameo glass; 1890–1900. *Left:* Tall vase; $350–450. *Right:* Squat vase; $300–375.

Tan and red cameo glass footed compote; by Charles Schnieder; 1890–1910; $650–775. This piece is in the Art Nouveau style.

Tan and green pate de verre bowl; by Amalric Walter; Nancy, France; 1910–15; $1,500–2,100. Walter specialized in pate de verre.

Small, green footed goblet; by Amalric Walter; Nancy, France; 1906–14; $900–1,200. In pate de verre technique, a mixture of crushed glass and colored oxides.

Enameled glass pitcher; by Emile Galle; Nancy, France; 1880–90; $1,000–1,350. Enameled glass has been known for centuries.

Enameled glass covered bowl; by Emile Galle; Nancy, France; 1900–10; $600–700.

Pair of vases in green glass decorated with purple and gold enamel; by Mont Joye Glass Co; France; 1900–10; $550–650.

Enameled glass; 1890–1910. *Left:* Sherbet bowl in blue and black; $100–125. *Right:* Cordial glass in red, green, and blue; $150–175.

Enameled glass vase in shades of blue; by Daum; Nancy, France; 1910–15; $750–875.

Enameled glass vase in blue, red, yellow, and white; by Leune; France; 1925–35; $150–200. A good example of Art Deco art glass.

Enameled glass sugar bowl and creamer in red and clear glass with gold trim; by Heisey Glass Co.; 1930–40; $65–90 the set.

Venetian glass vases in threaded white on orange and green glass; 1910–20; $140–180. Though first employed in Venice, the techniques of combining or "threading" contrasting colors of glass have been employed in many countries.

Frosted glass bowl
decorated in black and
yellow; by DeLatte;
Nancy, France; 1915–30;
$600–750.

English Nailsea-type pink and white
ribbed footed bowl; 1900–10; $80–110.
Nailsea was a major English center for
Venetian-type glass.

Clear and frosted glass
perfume decanter; by
Rene Lalique; 1920–30;
$500–600. Though best
known for his perfume
bottles, Lalique was a
major producer of many
types of frosted and cut
art glass.

Pair of Art Deco frosted glass
bookends; by Etling; France; 1930–40;
$350–425.

Pair of clear and frosted glass bud
vases mounted in sterling silver; 1910–
20; $275–325.

Art Deco cut-crystal
tumbler in clear and
cobalt blue glass; 1925–
35; $145–185.

Art Deco cut glass decorated in
black enamel; 1930–40. *Left:*
Ashtray; $60–90. *Right:*
Decanter; $125–175.

Cut-glass goblet engraved with a
forest scene in the Bohemian
manner; 1910–20; $110–145.

Spatter glass vase in shades of
red, blue, and green; by Charles
Schnieder; 1900–10; $500–575.
Multicolored spatter glass has
been produced in both Europe
and the United States.

Spatter glass vase in pink,
yellow, and white; 1920–30;
$175–225.

Art Deco glass; 1935–45. *Left:* Vase in pink and purple; $75–100. *Right:* Bud vase in clear glass and green; $40–60.

Spatter glass footed compote on pot-metal mounting; 1890–1900; $350–450. This piece, in shades of brown and yellow, is in the Art Nouveau style.

Vase with elaborate pastoral scene painted in enamels; 1880–1900; $435–470. Paintings of this sort were popular with the Victorians.

Clear glass figural liqueur bottles; 1925–35; $35–40 each. Made in molds, figural glass pieces are a popular form of art glass.

Clear glass figural candy bowl; 1930–40; $55–75.

Clear pressed-glass sherbet bowl; dated 1876; $50–80. Issued in commemoration of the centennial.

Art Deco lampshade in green and tan molded glass; 1920–30; $75–115.

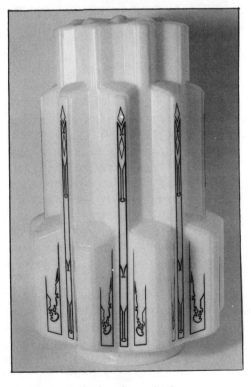

Art Deco milk glass lampshade decorated in black enamel; 1930–40; $85–135. Lampshades were so popular after the advent of electricity that even Tiffany made them.

Art Deco milk glass table lamp decorated in black enamel with a sheet tin base; 1925–35; $150–200.

Popular Glass

It is difficult for the modern collector, confronted with a blinding array of collectible glass, to realize that during most of the nineteenth century glass was a choice and expensive item.

The majority of this early glass was tediously hand formed, piece by piece. A glassblower would dip his hollow blowpipe into a vat of molten glass and remove a glob (called a gather) of glass. He would then expand and shape the gather by blowing through the pipe—in much the same way as a child blows a bubble. Because of the skill and time required, such glassware was always rather costly.

There had to be a better way—and there was. For hundreds of years glassmakers had employed molds, hollow wood or metal forms with designs carved into their interiors. A gather of glass made to expand within a form of this sort would retain the shape of the mold. It remained for American ingenuity to take the mold and make it the foundation of modern glass manufacture.

In 1825, John P. Bakewell of Pittsburgh patented an automatic pressing machine. No longer did the glassblower have to expand each gather of glass in a mold. The glass was fed automatically from the vat into a stamping machine where individual items were pressed out like cookies.

Spurred on by this innovation, American glassmakers began to produce a great quantity of housewares—cups, dishes, decanters, bowls, and the like—collectively known as pressed or pattern (from the decorative patterns embossed on their surfaces) glass.

The period of popularity of this pressed glass coincided in its later stages with the development of art glass, a fine, hand-formed and elaborately decorated ware (discussed in the preceding chapter). Unlike pressed glass, which was usually clear, art glass was brightly colored and of great appeal to the late Victorians.

It was only a matter of time before someone combined the best characteristics of pressed glass (inexpensiveness and mass production) with those of art glass (color and iridescence). When this was done (around 1905), the resulting ware was called iridescent art glass or opalescent glass. We know it better as carnival glass.

Carnival glass, like so many good ideas, was simple in concept. A piece of clear or colored pressed glass was sprayed with a liquid mixture of metallic salts and then refired. The finished ware would be covered with an exceptionally tough, multicolored coating of remarkable luster. In some cases this ware was so attractive that it was favorably compared to Tiffany favrile, leading to use of the name poor man's Tiffany when referring to carnival.

At present no less than one thousand different patterns exist in carnival, many of them recycled pressed-glass designs. The colors fall into two categories: strong hues, such as the very common orange or marigold, the cobalt blue, and the green; and pastels, such as pearly white, clambroth, gray, and pink.

The makers of carnival glass, attempting to satisfy every taste, employed numerous patterns. There are naturalistic designs, many of which echo the sinuous curves of Art Nouveau; geometric patterns employing variations of the straight line; stylized abstractions; and designs that imitate popular cut-glass patterns.

It should be noted that the name carnival glass was coined by collectors and refers to the ware's period of decline in the late 1920s, when unused stock was often given away as prizes at fairs and carnivals. But carnival glass was not inexpensive. In fact, contemporary price lists show that it was more expensive than pressed glass and that it was sold in the best shops.

Practically all carnival glass was made by one of four factories: the Fenton Art Glass Company, the Imperial Glass Company, the Millersburg Glass Company, and the Northwood Glass Company. Of these companies only Northwood marked its wares (with variations of the letter N), so most carnival glass must be identified by pattern alone.

The majority of carnival-glass collectors concentrate on the period from 1905 to 1925, but quite a bit of ware, almost all of it marigold hue, was made during the 1930s. This glass is known as late carnival. Also, within the past decade carnival has been reproduced by the Fenton Art Glass Company and the St. Clair Glassworks as well as by Imperial.

Popular as it was in its heyday, carnival never approached the universality of the pressed glass of the 1930s and 1940s. This ware, advertised as "sparkling dinnerware," is now known as Depression glass because of both its association with that era and the fact that, unlike carnival, it was inexpensive: it sold for as little as three cents apiece and was given away as a premium with cereal or at movie house "dish nights."

Unlike the iridescent carnival glass, Depression glass came in only some twenty-five different colors. These were both clear and opaque and ranged from the extremely common clear pink and pale green to such rarities as ruby red, smoke gray, and opaque blue.

There are also fewer Depression-glass patterns than carnival patterns. At present only some ninety-five are known, and these can be divided into three distinguishable types. The first is mold etched, in which the piece is lightly stippled in semihigh-relief patterns, usually floral. Examples illustrated here are in the Adam and Florentine patterns. Less commonly seen are traditional molded patterns in which the design is formed by the shape and contour of the glass. The third type is chip molded, in which the overall pattern appears to be cut or chipped as it is in cut glass. Examples shown here are in the Sharon pattern.

All three pattern types are attractive, but the mold-etched variety is particularly popular with collectors, many of whom do not realize that it was often employed because the stippling helped to disguise the numerous bubbles and flaws found in cheap glass.

As with carnival, Depression glass is chiefly collected by pattern, though the ultimate goal is to obtain a complete set in a desirable color, such as cobalt blue or deep green. Such an ambition is complicated by the fact that within a given pattern and hue certain pieces are usually much harder to find than others. Saucers, plates, and creamers, for example, are relatively easy to come by; but such things as covered butter dishes, cookie jars, and handled sandwich servers may require a long hunt and substantial expense.

The great bulk of all Depression glass was made by eight companies: the Anchor Hocking Glass Company, the Jeannette Glass Company, the Indiana Glass Company, the Hazel Atlas Glass Company, the MacBeth-Evans Glass Company, the U.S. Glass Company, the Imperial Glass Company, and the Federal Glass Company. Researchers have been able to trace most Depression glass patterns to one or more of these plants.

It is also important to know that pieces may be generally dated by color. For example, pinks and greens were made from 1926 to 1940, yellows were produced between 1930 and 1934, and cobalts were produced only in 1936 and 1937. Amethysts were made in a single year, 1935, teal only in 1937, and ruby in 1940.

Though prices have risen during the last decade, Depression glass remains one of the most accessible and inexpensive of all twentieth-century collectibles. Vast quantities were produced, and even today it is possible to obtain a sizable collection with a minimum expense.

Throughout the first half of this century, many other types of collectible glass were manufactured in the United States. Much of this ware was of a higher quality than is generally associated with Depression glass. The A. H. Heisey Glass Company, in business from 1896 until 1957, produced a wide variety of fine pressed glass, and its products are now considered extremely desirable. Another company whose wares are much sought after is the Cambridge Glass Company, active from 1901 through 1954.

The Imperial Glass Company and several other manufacturers created an unusual and popular form—called stretch glass—during the 1930s. This frosted and richly curvilinear glass is found in several colors, including red, green, blue, and yellow. Because its lines go well with modern furnishings stretch glass is rapidly becoming a collector's favorite.

Extremely fine blown and etched tablewares have been made since 1887 by the Fostoria Glass Company. Fostoria wineglasses and tumblers are particularly prized for their fine designs and delicate forms. In recent years there has been growing interest in the products of the New Martinsville Glass Company, Libby, Steuben, and many others. Indeed, there are few twentieth-century factories whose wares have passed unnoticed by collectors.

Another growing field is that of modern, machine-made bottles. The invention of the automatic bottle-making machine in 1906 sounded the death knell for the traditional craft of glassblowing, and for many collectors 1906 marks the termination point of their bottle-collecting interests. However, rising prices for earlier bottles have forced collectors to look more favorably on later vessels. These can be distinguished from nineteenth-century examples by the fact that the mold marks on their necks run completely over the lip of the bottle rather than terminating somewhere along the neck.

Many unusual and interesting bottles, in both clear and colored glass, have been made since 1906, and prices for the most part remain relatively low. Popular types at present are beer and milk bottles, fruit jars and whiskies, but almost any twentieth-century vessel is potentially collectible.

Iridescent green carnival glass footed bowl in Louwesa pattern; $55–70. A popular pattern and color.

Carnival glass. *Left:* Orange vase in panel and loop pattern; $30–45. *Center:* Green vase in ripple pattern; $45–55. *Right:* Orange vase in diamondpoint pattern; $35–45. Vases are among the most common pieces of carnival glass.

Pair of smoky yellow carnival glass candleholders in vertical panel pattern; $40–55. From 1905 to 1925 carnival glass provided an inexpensive substitute for art glass.

Left and *Right:* Purple carnival glass punch cups in acorn pattern; $35–45 each. *Center:* Purple whiskey tumbler in grape and cable pattern; $165–200. The whiskey tumbler is a rare piece.

Peach opalescent carnival glass fruit bowl; $60–85.

Blue Phoenix glass vase with white floral design in relief; $55–65. Though not true art glass, Phoenix, like carnival, offered an inexpensive substitute for the one-of-a-kind pieces.

Phoenix glass. *Left:* Large pale blue flattened vase with white floral design in relief; $60–85. *Center:* Small yellow bowl; $10–15. *Right:* Flat purple vase; $25–35.

Adam pattern Depression glass. *Left:* Pink divided relish dish; $6–10. *Center left:* Pink pitcher; $15–20. *Center right:* Green dessert bowl; 3–6. *Right:* Green tumbler; $6–9. Made in many different colors and patterns, Depression glass was widely manufactured during the 1930s and 1940s. ▼

Cameo pattern Depression glass; by Anchor Hocking Glass Co. *Left:* Pale yellow grill plate; $4–6. *Right:* Pale green platter; $6–8. A delicate lacy pattern, cameo is popular with collectors. ▼

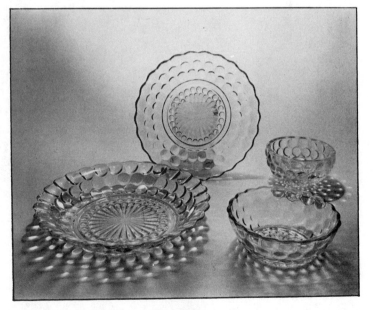

Bubble pattern Depression glass; by Anchor Hocking Glass Co. *Rear left:* Salad dish; $1–3. *Rear right:* Candleholder; $3–6. *Front left:* Soup bowl; $3–5. *Front right:* Cereal bowl; $3–5. All pieces pale blue. One of the more common patterns, bubble represents a good investment for the beginning collector.

Colonial pattern Depression glass. *Left:* Pink pitcher; $25–32. *Center:* Pink shot glass; $4–7. *Right:* Clear covered butter dish; $25–38. Colonial is similar in style to 19th-century American pressed glass. ◄

Cubist pattern Depression glass. *Left:* ▲ Candy jar; $10–17. *Center:* Serving bowl; $6–9. *Right:* Powder jar; $10–15. All pieces pink. Its modern look has endeared cubist to many enthusiasts.

◄ Florentine pattern Depression glass. *Left:* Green tumbler; $4–7. *Left rear:* Topaz salad dish; $2–4. *Center rear:* Pink ruffled footed compote $7–10. *Right rear:* Green cream soup bowl; $7–12. *Front:* Pink vegetable bowl; $8–15.

Floral pattern Depression glass; by Jeannette Glass Co. *Left:* Green divided relish dish; $7–13. *Center:* Pink covered vegetable dish; $10–15. *Right:* Green sherbet dish; $5–7. Floral is a common and popular pattern.

Forest green pattern Depression glass. *Left:* Tubular vase; $3–5. *Center:* Large, patterned vase; $9–15. *Right:* Bud vase; $2–5. All pieces deep green. Forest green is a lovely and underpriced pattern.

◄ Iris pattern Depression glass; by Jeannette Glass Co. *Left:* Double candlestick $8–17. *Center left:* Large vase; $10–16. *Center right:* Wine goblet; $10–14. *Right:* Footed tumbler; $8–12. All pieces clear. Another very attractive and moderately priced pattern.

Floragold pattern Depression glass,
Left: Pink and gold salad bowl; $9–13.
Center: Pink dogwood creamer; $2–4.
Right: Dusky pink lace-edged serving
bowl; $5–8.

Madrid pattern Depression glass; by
Federal Glass Co. *Left:* Covered sugar
bowl; $10–15. *Center:* Handled cream
soup bowl; $5–8. *Right:* Pitcher; $18–
26. *Rear:* Console bowl; $8–13. All
pieces amber.

Mayfair pattern Depression glass. *Left:*
Clear pitcher; $8–15. *Center:* Pink cake
plate; $10–15. *Right:* Pink decanter;
$35–45. Decanters are extremely rare
in Depression glass. The price for this
one would double in a more popular
pattern.

Moderntone pattern Depression glass;
by Hazel Atlas Glass Co. *Left:*
Amethyst cup and saucer; $8–13.
Center: Cobalt blue salt and pepper
shakers; $20–25. *Right:* Cobalt blue
Jell-O bowl; $5–9. This pattern is
especially favored by fanciers of Art
Deco.

Moonstone pattern Depression glass.
Rear left: Clear and opalescent cologne
bottle; $10–17. *Center rear:* Handled
serving bowl; $8–14. *Right rear:* Vase;
$7–11. *Front:* Pair of candlesticks;
$16–24.

113

Mount Pleasant pattern Depression glass. *Left:* Footed sherbet bowl. $7–11; *Center:* Double candlestick; $13–21. *Right:* Three-footed bowl; $15–25. All pieces cobalt blue with gold banding. Cobalt is one of the most popular glass colors.

▲

Patrician pattern Depression glass. *Left:* Green handled cream soup bowl; $5–8. *Center:* Amber covered cookie jar; $25–35. *Right:* Amber covered butter dish; $40–60. Patrician is one of the most favored Depression glass patterns.

Princess pattern Depression glass; by Anchor Hocking Glass Co. *Left:* Heart-shaped bowl; $10–15. *Center:* Footed tumbler; $12–18. *Right:* Oval vegetable dish; $8–13. All pieces pink.

Royal lace pattern Depression glass. *Left:* Pink tumbler; $6–7. *Center:* Blue plate; $9–11. *Right:* Pink covered cookie jar; $15–18. This is another popular pattern with good investment potential. ▶

Sandwich pattern Depression glass *Left:* Clear open sugar bowl; by Duncan Mills; $8–12. *Center:* Clear cookie jar; by Anchor Hocking Glass Co.; $15–22. *Right:* Dark green tumbler; by Anchor Hocking Glass Co.; $5–8. *Front:* Green bowl; by Anchor Hocking Glass Co.; $4–7.

Sharon pattern Depression glass; by Indiana Glass Co. *Left:* Amber candy dish; $13–18. *Center:* Fruit bowl; $8–12. *Right:* Handled cream soup bowl; $7–11. Though not uncommon, amber is one of the more popular Depression glass hues.

Shell pink pattern Depression glass. *Left:* Snack set; $5–8. *Center:* Footed fruit bowl; $7–11. *Right:* Covered box; $9–14. All pieces opaque pink. Though generally less popular than clear glass, opaque Depression ware is attracting increasing attention.

Miss America pattern Depression glass; by Anchor Hocking Glass Co. *Left* and *Right:* Clear glass cream and sugar bowls; $10–15 the pair. *Center:* Pink platter; $9–14.

English hobnail pattern Depression glass; by Westmorland Glass Co. Milk glass lamp base; $40–58. Depression glass lamp bases are not common.

Cherry delfite pattern Depression glass; by Jeannette Glass Co. *Left:* Tumbler; $15–24. *Center* and *Right:* Cream and sugar bowls; $25–35 the pair. *Front:* Platter; $28–25. All pieces in opaque pale blue glass.

Jane Ray's jadite pattern Depression glass; by McKee Glass Co. Plate; $1–3. Cup and saucer; $2–4. All pieces in opaque sea green glass. This pattern is substantially undervalued.

Laurel pattern Depression glass; by McKee Glass Co. *Left* and *right:* Pair of candlesticks; $20–30. *Center:* Covered cheese plate; $35–48. All pieces in French ivory.

Doric and pansy pattern Depression glass. *Left* and *right:* Sherbet bowls; $4–6 each. *Center:* Bonbon dish; $7–10. All pieces in delphi blue. This lovely pattern should increase rapidly in value.

AKRO agate Depression glass. *Left:* Miniature white creamer; $3–5; green concentric ring dish; $2–4. *Center rear:* Blue and white planter; $5–9. *Center front:* Green octagonal plate; $5–8. *Right:* White octagonal plate; $2–4. Children's toy dish sets in AKRO agate are particularly in demand.

Sportsmen's Series glass *Left:* Sailboat tumbler; $5–7. *Center left:* Fish juice glass; $2–5 *Center right:* Fox hunter cocktail shaker; $15–22. *Right:* Skier ice bowl; $10–15. All pieces with transfer decoration on dark blue glass. This 1930s-era ware was intended for the game room or cocktail lounge.

Red glass cocktail set flashed in silver; $135–165. Well-designed sets of this sort date to the 1930s and reflect the modernistic designs of Art Deco.

Left: Vase; $5–10. *Center left:* Cocktail shaker; $25–35. *Center right:* Bud vase; $3–5. *Right:* Clear-top covered storage container; $7–11. All pieces are ruby glass, a popular and inexpensive 1930s glass.

Clear glass punch bowl set; by Heisey Glass Co. Bowl and stand; 1930–40. $165–200. Punch cups; 1930–40; $5–10 each. During its sixty-one years of existence the Heisey plant turned out a great quantity of collectible glass.

Left: Pink glass pickle dish; $15–20. *Right:* Clear pressed-glass hair receiver with electroplated silver top; $35–45. Both by Heisey Glass Co.; 1930–40.

Left: Frosted glass bonbon tray; $12–15. *Right:* Clear and frosted glass cocktail pitcher with stainless steel mountings; 1930–40.; $70–80. Two examples of better-quality depression-era glass.

Stanhope pattern glass; Heisey Glass Co. *Left* and *center:* Cream and sugar bowls; $35–50 the pair. *Right:* Cup and saucer; $15–20. All are examples of Art Deco design. The fittings are in hard plastic.

Left and *right:* Pair of amber and clear glass cruets; $15–22. *Center:* Amber footed compote in chrome mounting; $25–38. All by Cambridge Glass Co. Though of fairly recent vintage, Cambridge is popular among collectors.

Purple footed compote in the Art Nouveau manner; by Cambridge Glass Co.; $65–105. The chrome mountings are by Farber Brothers.

Clear crystal glass candleholder in the form of a flying sea gull; by Cambridge Glass Co.; $35–50.

Purple and clear glass pitcher; by Cambridge Glass Co.; $50–75. An extremely fine example of stylish 20th-century utilitarian glass.

Left: Small purple bowl; $3–6. *Center:* Dark purple fan vase; $20–30. *Right:* Dark purple serving bowl; $18–28. All by New Martinsville Glass Co.

Pink and clear glass wineglasses and goblets; by Fostoria Glass Co.; $ 15–25 each. All are in the pink Versailles pattern.

Stretch glass. Pair of matte green candleholders with white ribbing; $65–90. The rich colors of stretch glass made it one of the most popular mass-produced answers to art glass.

Stretch glass. *Left:* Bowl; $75–110. *Center:* Tall vase; $150–200. *Right:* Vase; $140–180. All pieces in various shades of red. Red is one of the less common colors in this glass.

Stretch glass in vaseline finish. *Left:* Fan vase; $22–26. *Center:* Cake plate with clear handle; $30–34. *Right:* Footed rose bowl; $35–38.

Stretch glass in shades of blue; 1930–40. *Left:* Eight-sided footed vase; $20–30. *Center rear:* Tall compote; by Imperial Glass Co.; $50–65. *Center front:* Footed compote; $25–35. *RightFluted vase; $35–50.*

Pink satin glass lamp, shade, and powder box combination; 1930–40. $75–115.

Pair of white milk glass kitchen salt and pepper shakers with metal tops; 1940–50; $15–20. Dispensers such as these are also found in sea green glass.

Set of clear glass kitchen dispensers spray-painted red and blue with red and green tin tops; 1940–50; $55–70. *Left:* Set of catsup or oil dispensers. *Center:* Pair of salt and pepper shakers. *Right: :* Sugar cannisters.

Cherry pattern pressed-glass tumblers with enameled decoration; $10–15 each. Good-quality glass of the period 1920 to 1930.

Cut-glass whiskey decanter in clear crystal with black and pink enamel; $65–95. Because it was always more expensive there is less existing cut glass from the period 1920 to 1930 than pressed glass.

Cut-glass dressing table set and tray in the Art Deco mode; 1930–40; $165–225.

Left: Amber whiskey bottle; $2–4. *Center left:* Pale blue medicine bottle; $3–5. *Center right:* Lime green Royall Lyme bottle; $2–4. *Right:* Cobalt blue "eye water" bottle with applicator; $15–25. The Royall Lyme bottle is a 1960s reproduction already acquiring status with collectors.

Left: Light green Atlas E-Z Seal fruit jar; $2–4. *Center:* Amber cod-liver-oil bottle in the shape of a fish; $10–15. *Right:* Clear castor-oil bottle with original contents; $8–12. Common 20th-century bottle glass. Machine-made 20th-century bottles are just beginning to attract collector attention.

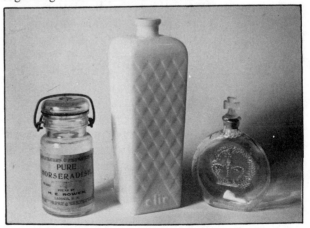

Left: Clear horseradish bottle; $3–5. *Center:* Milk glass case gin bottle; $25–35. *Right:* Clear embossed cologne bottle; $15–25. All these 20th-century bottles are completely machine made.

Silver

Although there were American silversmiths active as early as the seventeenth century, only a relatively small amount of pre-1860 silver is available, and what can be found is invariably high priced. This is because until the discovery of Nevada's Comstock Lode in 1858 there was practically no native silver bullion available.

Following the Civil War, major silver manufacturers in Massachusetts, Connecticut, and New York began to turn out a bewildering variety of forms, all designed to cater to the tastes of an expanding and opulent middle class.

One of the first in the field was Charles Lewis Tiffany (1812 to 1902), father of the famous glassmaker. The elder Tiffany was in business by 1860, won a prize at the Paris Exposition of 1867, and by 1890 headed the largest silver factory in the world. In 1893, at the height of its prominence, the Tiffany firm held appointments to twenty-three crowned heads of state, including Queen Victoria and the Czar of Russia.

Tiffany is by far the most popular silverware of the late nineteenth and early twentieth centuries. In style it varies from early Victorian eclectic to Art Nouveau, with pieces in the latter mode regarded as most typical. The Tiffany output was enormous and varied—everything from hatpins to gigantic commemorative centerpieces is available. There is a great deal of flatware, including such oddities as baby feeders and napkin holders as well as objects of adornment ranging from brooches to belt buckles.

Tiffany concentrated on sterling silver, which is 92.5 percent pure ore, and the combination of weight and reputation assures that Tiffany's products are expensive collector's items. There are many other makers, however, such as the Meriden Silver Company of Meriden, Connecticut, which manufactured less-expensive electroplated silver. Electroplate is produced by passing an electric current through a silver solution, which causes the silver to adhere to bars of copper or pewter submerged in the liquid. The result is a thin coating of silver over the base metal—a much less expensive product. Late-nineteenth- and early-twentieth-century electroplate is often elaborate to the point of tastelessness, but well-designed examples can be found, and they represent a good investment. One should choose only specimens that show minimal wear—otherwise one must be prepared to undergo the expense of resilvering. Electroplate with the dull red glow of copper showing through the plating is not a particularly attractive acquisition.

Another major American maker of both sterling and electroplate was the Gorham Manufacturing Company of Providence, Rhode Island. Established in 1831, Gorham began producing silver in 1871, when it brought over the famous English designer William T. Codman, who developed the distinctive line of hammered silver known as martele and the sophisticated Art Nouveau style called athenic. During its long existence, Gorham has turned out much fine silver, including a variety of flatware, serving pieces, trinket boxes, vases, whiskey flasks, cigarette cases, inkwells, and complete tea and coffee sets.

Unger Brothers was a manufacturer with a more limited output than Tiffany or Gorham, but its ware is in great demand today. Unger was active in New Jersey from 1881 to 1910 — the period of his greatest productivity coincided with the height of the Art Nouveau movement—and the company is famous for teaspoons, dresser sets (matching mirror, brush, and comb), belt buckles, and doorknobs decorated with the profiles of young women with long, flowing hair. Marked U.B., Unger Brothers ware is highly collectible and still somewhat underpriced.

As the twentieth century advanced, major producers such as Reed and Barton and the International Silver Company dominated the field, and much of their ware made during the period from 1910 to 1940 lacks creativity. However, there were a number of individual silversmiths and small firms active in large cities, and sophisticated collectors are now seeking out their products. Sterling by such makers as Pier Smed (active in New York City, from circa 1830 to circa 1835) and Dominick and Haff (active in New York City, from circa 1888 to circa 1890) is well made and attractively styled. It is also just the sort of thing that may be overlooked by dealers and collectors bent on acquiring a piece of marked Tiffany or Gorham. In this, as in every area, knowledge pays!

Nor should one overlook the fine Art Nouveau and Art Deco silver manufactured abroad and imported into this country. Such makers as W. H. Haseler of Birmingham, England—manufacturer of the famous cymric pattern sold by Liberty from 1899 until well into the 1920s—produced quality ware that has been used and collected in this country for decades. There is also the famous Danish silversmith Georg Jensen. The ware he made while in his native land is among the finest produced in this century; but some collectors are not aware that during the Second World War he established himself in this country, and it is possible to obtain American-made Jensen silver.

The styles of collectible silver are many and varied. Before the turn of the century, Art Nouveau was dominant, but Tiffany, Gorham, and the electroplate manufacturers turned out pieces in many other highly eclectic Victorian modes, such as Egyptian Revival, Renaissance, and Gothic. After 1900, certain manufacturers returned temporarily to the slim lines and simple shapes of the neoclassic, but by the 1920s, Art Deco had taken hold. The geometric forms and strong, definite shapes characteristic of this mode prevailed until well into the 1940s.

Because silver is a valuable metal, collectors must anticipate paying for weight as well as form. Therefore, larger pieces in any style are always expensive. Beginning collectors or those of modest means should look for small pieces with interesting form and decoration. Such things as comb and pencil cases, belt buckles, spoons, perfume flasks, table bells, match safes, and sewing paraphernalia can often be purchased inexpensively. Moreover, because most silver manufacturers marked their ware, it is possible to find items bearing the coveted ciphers of Tiffany, Gorham, or Unger.

When seeking out silver, bear in mind that experts agree that compared to European examples, American-made silver remains underpriced in today's inflated antiques market. As such it offers the rare combination of both a beautiful acquisition and a practical investment.

Covered serving dish; by Charles Lewis Tiffany; 1880–90; $900–1,150. Tiffany was the dean of late-19th-century silver makers.

Footed serving tray with enamel decoration; by Tiffany Studios; 1920–25; $500–650.

Covered box; by Tiffany Studios; 1920–25; $175–225.

Powder boxes; 1900–10. *Left:* By Tiffany Studios; $175–220. *Right:* $160–200.

Left: Powder box; by Tiffany Studios; 1900–10; $125–155. *Center:* Belt buckle; by Tiffany Studios; ca. 1900; $65–95. *Right:* Art Nouveau whiskey flask; 1890–1900; $200–275.

Sewing tools; 1880–1920. *Top left:* Pincushion; $15–25. *Center left:* Bobbin; $30–50. *Bottom left:* Thimble; $20–25. *Center:* Thread holder; $110–120. *Top right:* Bobbin sheath; $65–80. *Bottom right:* Darning egg; signed by Charles Lewis Tiffany; $170–210.

Set of teaspoons; by Baker Silver Co.; 1890–1900; $30–40 each. *Center:* Bonbon spoon; by Tiffany Studios; 1885–95; $85–115.

Napkin holders; 1885–1930. *Left:* By Tiffany Studios; $80–115. *Center left:* $40–50. *Center right:* 70–95. *Right:* 100–140.

Hot-water reservoir; by Gorham Silver Co.; ca. 1892; $1,00–1,350.

Tea set; by Gorham Silver Co.; 1900–05; $5,000–6,500. This choice set is in the hammered martele style developed by Gorham's William Codman.

Tea set; by Gorham Silver Co.; 1895–1905; $1,000–1,400.

Pierced bonbon bowl; by
Gorham Silver Co.; 1910–20;
$85–135.

Utensils; 1890–1910. *Top:* Fish
fork; by Shiebler Silver Co.; $30–
40. *Top center:* Teaspoon; by
Shiebler Silver Co., $20–30.
Bottom center: Seafood spoon;
by Gorham Silver Co; $30–40.
Bottom: Seafood fork; by   ▼
Wallace Silver Co.; $35–45.

Athenic pattern vase; by Gorham
Silver Co.; 1900–15; $700–950.
Designed by William Codman.

Art Nouveau trinket box; by
Gorham Silver Co.; 1900–05;
$165–215.

Heart-shaped trinket box; by
Gorham Silver Co.; 1900–05;
$70–95.

Left: Whiskey flask; 1900–10; $185–235. *Center:* Perfume flask; dated 1909; $115–145. *Right:* Perfume flask; by Gorham Silver Co.; 1900–10; $185–225.

Top: Art Deco whiskey flask; by Gorham Silver Co.; 1930–40; $115–135. *Bottom:* Whiskey flask; by International Silver Co.; 1940–50; $110–140.

Inkwell; by Gorham Silver Co.; 1920–25; $240–290. The glass fount is by Pairpont Glass Co.

Ashtray and match holder; by Gorham Silver Co.; 1900–05; $105–135. This piece, which was probably used in a yacht club, is inlaid with enamel in blue and green.

Unusual cigar case; by Gorham Silver Co.; 1880–85; $140–175.

Art Nouveau spoons; by Unger Brothers Silver Co.; 1905–10; $25–40.

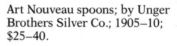

Left: Cigarette case and matching comb case; $350–400 the pair. *Bottom:* Brooch; $30–40. *Right:* Bracelet; $275–325. All by Unger Brothers Silver Co.; 1890–1915.

Baby cup; by Reed and Barton; 1920–25; $55–75.

Flagon or tall cup; signed and dated by Pier Smed; 1934; $3,000–4,000. Smed's work is relatively uncommon.

Cigar lighter in the shape of a candlestick; by Dominick and Haff; 1880–90; $145–195. The surface of this piece is hammered in a manner similar to that employed by Gorham during the same period.

Pitcher; by Dominick and Haff; ca. 1881; $675–800.

Bamboo pattern tea set; by Bisanda; 1900–20; $1,000–1,500. This set weighs forty-two ounces

Mug; by Ball, Black & Co.; ca. 1880; $165–210.

Cymric pattern flagon; by
Liberty Manufacturing
Co.; ca. 1905; $9,000–
12,000. An extremely rare
piece.

Art Deco tea set; 1925–35;
$1,500–2,000.

Child's dinner set; 1890–
1900; $350–450.

Beaker; 1910–15; $65–85.
Beakers of this sort were usually
made in sets.

Silver and copper drinking mug
in the Arts and Crafts mode;
dated 1903. Inscribed " 'My only
books were women's looks and
folly all they taught me.' From a
girl in Paris."

Baby spoons; 1890–1920; $45–75 each.

Dinner-table bells; 1880–1930; $65–135. Servants' bells were customary in some homes until the late 1930s.

Art Deco box; by Alphonse LaPaglia; ca. 1925; $185–235.

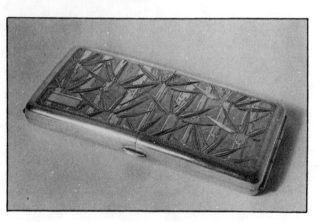

Cigarette case; 1930–35; $250–320.

Art Nouveau visiting-card case; 1890–1900; $235–315.

Pressed-glass dresser bottles with sterling silver tops; 1890–1910. *Left to right:* $70–95; $40–65; $60–75; $35–55; $75–115.

Cut-glass dresser or vanity bottles with sterling silver tops; 1890–1910. *Left:* $55–75. *Right:* $85–125. ▶

Left: Paneled perfume flask; 1890–1920; $115–145. *Center top:* Silver overlay whiskey flask; 1890–1920; $200–275. *Center bottom:* Art Nouveau flask; 1890–1920; $180–230. *Right:* Silver and crystal flask; dated 1902; $75–100.

Nut dish with goat's head finial on the handle; 1880–90; $165–235.

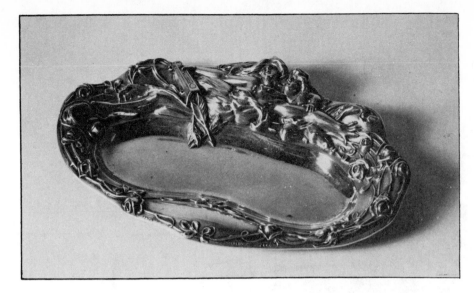

Art Nouveau card tray; 1890–1905; $175–225.

Match safes; 1890–1920. *Left:* Art Nouveau; $70–90. *Center:* $45–60. *Right:* $50–75.

Cigarette case decorated with golfer in black enamel; 1920–25; $125–155.

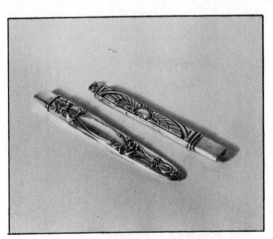

Left: Art Nouveau sealing-wax seal; 1900–05; $90–100. *Right:* Sealing-wax seal; 1910–15; $80–90. Even as late as the 1920s many people sealed their letters with wax, using initialed seals.

Pencil holders; 1910–20. *Left:* $50–65. *Right:* $50–65. These holders protected small, flat pencils of a sort rarely seen today.

133

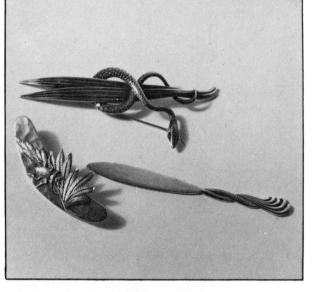

Left: Silver chatelaine with gold insert; 1890–1900; $140–180. *Right:* Belt buckle; 1890–1900; $100–135. Chatelaines were worn on the belt to hold keys and similar items.

Sterling silver accessories; 1890–1930. *Left bottom:* Baby rattle; $120–155. *Left top:* Rouge box; $55–70. *Center top:* Bottle corker; $70–95. *Right:* Dance pad; $85–115.

Left: Brooch; 1910–20; $100–135. *Top:* Unusual snake brooch; 1900–05; $185–225. *Right:* Letter opener; 1890–1900; $70–95.

Picture frame; 1945–50; $110–140. Intended for use with a baby picture.

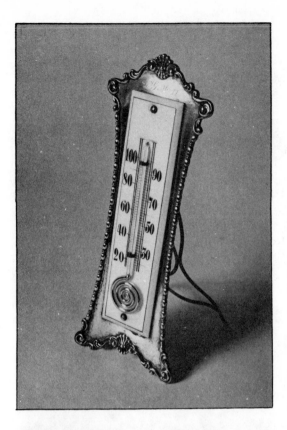

Porcelain thermometer with stand; 1910–15; $120–155.

Bowl; by Georg Jensen; New York, N.Y.; 1940–45; $350–450.

Pair of electroplated vases; 1890–1900; $100–145. Less expensive than sterling, silver plate swept the United States in the second half of the 19th century.

Electroplated tea set; 1930–35; $200–275. This stylish set is in the Art Deco mode.

Electroplated nut dish; 1910–20; $55–70.

Electroplated Art Nouveau lift-top box; 1890–1900; $65–85.

Electroplated bud-vase stand with cut- and engraved-glass insert; 1890–1900; $75–115.

Electroplated Art Nouveau card tray; 1880–1900; $650–850. A high quality of craftsmanship is displayed in this fine piece.

Electroplated card tray; 1890–1900; $115–155.

Electroplated card tray; 1880–1900;
$85–120.

Electroplated ashtray with pressed-
glass bowl; 1925–35; $125–150.

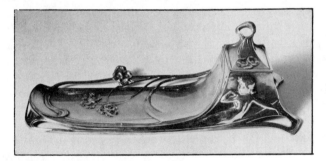

Electroplated inkwell; 1890–1905;
$135–170. The elongated form and
swirling surface decoration are typical
of Art Nouveau design.

Electroplated paper-
weight; 1890–1900; $165–
245.

Electroplated sailing
trophy; dated 1925; $85–
135. Pieces of this sort
usually have more historical than aesthetic interest

Bronze

Collectible bronze can be divided into two general categories: the purely decorative sculptural pieces, including figures or busts of humans and animals; and the utilitarian items that, though they too may incorporate figural elements, are intended primarily to serve a function. These latter range from floor lamps and ash stands to tiny seals used in correspondence.

Traditionally, only the sculptural pieces were regarded as worthy of collection, and because they were generally one of a kind—were, in fact, works of art—they were expensive even when new. However, late in the nineteenth century advanced technology made possible the issuance of hundreds—even thousands—of duplicate pieces based on a single master figure. *Bronzes d'edition* as they were known in France, enabled the sculptor to reach an audience that had previously been unable to afford his work.

These multiple editions have proved a mixed blessing to the collector, for the work of many late-nineteenth- and early-twentieth-century sculptors has been reissued so many times that the later editions are no better than reproductions. Figural bronzes by major artists are expensive, and it behooves the collector to know his field or to buy from a reputable dealer. The presence of an artist's signature in no way guarantees that a piece is not a recent casting.

Bronze is an alloy containing approximately eighty-eight parts copper and twelve parts tin, though zinc or lead may be added to vary color or strength. In an untarnished state the metal appears reddish brown, and with age it acquires a blue green, gray, or black patina. Because bronze is easily cast, most collectible objects are made in that manner.

Since the 1880s, most casting has been done in large foundries, such as the Barbedienne in Paris and New York's Roman Bronze Works. The techniques developed in these shops are largely responsible for the proliferation of bronze art in the past century.

Today's collector can choose from literally hundreds of different figural bronzes ranging from reproductions of Renaissance works to Art Deco pieces produced in the 1920s and 1930s. Quality varies greatly. Even the most recent versions of masterworks are preferable to some of the Victorian-period pieces, which were created solely to capitalize on a fashion or to mimic the style of a well-known sculptor. One must make careful choices, and personal taste or professional advice will prove the key to wise investment.

There are certain artists whose work is always a desirable acquisition. American collectors are constantly seeking examples by the great painter and sculptor of the West, Frederic Remington. Remington executed his first bronze in 1895, and before his death in 1910 he produced several dozen excellent renditions of cowboys, Indians, and western animals. Remington bronzes have been widely reproduced.

European bronzes popular among American collectors include the work of Les Animaliers as well as the works of those sculptors who specialized in representations of contemporary actresses and dancers. Les Animaliers was a group of sculptors, headed by the renowned Antoine Louis Barye (1795 to 1875), who prided themselves on anatomically correct renderings of animal forms. Their work, which was at its height during the period between 1890 and 1915, was generally of small scale and was naturalistic and highly detailed. Bronzes by Barye and his successors Georges Gardet and François Pompon now bring high prices.

Quite a different group were those sculptors, such as the Frenchman Raoul Larche, who cast likenesses of the great entertainers of the day—women like the dancer Looi Fuller and the actress Sarah Bernhardt. The work of these artists was much more traditional in mood than that of Les Animaliers, and it exploited fully the Art Nouveau preoccupation with female nudes. Though out of style since early in the century, these pieces are making a comeback.

Figural pieces represent only a small portion of the bronze available to present-day collectors. There are also the utilitarian objects. Everything from mirror and picture frames to doorstops and lamp bases has been cast in bronze, and it's all collectible. Moreover, much of the best is American made.

As in the fields of glass and silver, the name Tiffany is important. Louis Comfort Tiffany began experimenting with metalwares in the 1890s and soon developed a fondness for bronze. By 1901 his bronze lamp bases were winning awards at the Buffalo Exposition.

Before 1900, Tiffany bronze was stamped T. G. & D. CO. (Tiffany Glass and Decorating Company). After that year, the Tiffany Studios mark was used. Like most of his other products, Tiffany metal is usually marked.

Bronze can be colored through the application of chemicals, and Tiffany Studios employed four such basic patinas: dark green, golden bronze, brown, and pure gold. The ware, which numbered dozens of different objects—from candlesticks and figurines to inkwells and letter openers—was made in several characteristic patterns, the most popular of which were those known as pine bough, grape vine, and zodiac. Though hardly in-expensive, Tiffany bronze is within the reach of most collectors and offers an interesting field—if only because of the large variety of objects produced. It is possible, for example, to assemble a substantial collection of different Tiffany candlesticks or desk sets.

Tiffany Studios was not the only manufacturer of bronze accessories during the early twentieth century. The Revere Studios, another major producer, made ware in a pattern so similar to grape vine that, though properly marked, it is frequently confused with the more desirable Tiffany.

The Roycrafters, of East Aurora, New York, made bronze candlesticks, bookends, and ink-wells in the Arts and Crafts manner. These pieces, which are sometimes marked BRADLEY & HUBBARD, are eagerly sought as complements to Mission-style furniture. Many other companies, not all of which marked their products, made bronze ware, particularly writing implements. The abundance of these, particularly inkwells and writing boxes, is explained by the fact that the expansion of literacy at the close of the nineteenth century combined with the institution of universal penny postage in 1898 led to a great increase in letter writing. Much of the equipment that was manufactured to fill the need for writing materials remains today to fill the need for collectibles.

Small bronze incense holder; 1940–50; $15–20.

Figure of a youth; by Raoul Larche; 1890–1905; $700–950. A sculptor in the classic tradition, Larche made castings of actresses and dancers that are in great demand.

Figure of a woman; by Tiffany Studios; 1910–20; $175–235. One of a set of bookends, this piece is typical of the whimsical figures produced by the Tiffany shop.

Figure of the goddess Astarte; 1890–95; $500–750.

Figure of a discus thrower; by R. Tate McKenzie; ca. 1929; $1,400–1,900.

Figure of Diana the huntress and deer, set in marble; 1930–35; $175–255. A typical example of unsigned factory-produced bronze.

Bust of Shakespeare; by A. Carri-
ere; 1895–1905; $650–750.

Art Nouveau bust of a young
woman; 1890–1900; $200–325.

Bust of George Washington;
1910–20; $175–250. As in the
19th century, 20th-century sculptors produced many figures of
early patriots such as Washington, Adams, and Lincoln.

Relief sculpture of a young
woman and man; by Ruth
Milles; 1910–20; $900–1,350.

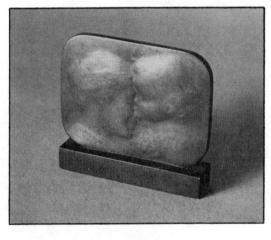

Tiny relief sculpture of mother
and child; 1900–10; $135–175.

Bust, possibly of U. S. Grant; 1890–
1900; $150–180.

Relief sculpture of a young woman; by
Theodad; 1920–30; $200–275.

Trophy plaque for Spalding Olympic;
dated 1925; $95–145.

Miniature head; 1890–1910; $35–45.

Sculpture of a lion and python; by
Antoine Louis Barye; ca. 1890; $700–
950.

Sculpture of two deer; by P. Camolero;
1910–20; $1,400–1,850.

Sculpture of a dog; by
Louise Allen; dated 1914;
$400–650.

Stylized miniature figure
of a dog; by Haganauer;
1930–40; $80–125.

Sculpture of a dog; 1905–
15; $125–175.

Miniature animals; 1900–
20. *Left:* Bear; $25–35.
Center: Duck; $15–20.
Right: Penguin; $25–35.

Art Nouveau card tray; 1930–35;
$100–175. Stamped on the back is
"Diamond Jim Brady Room, Luchow's
New York."

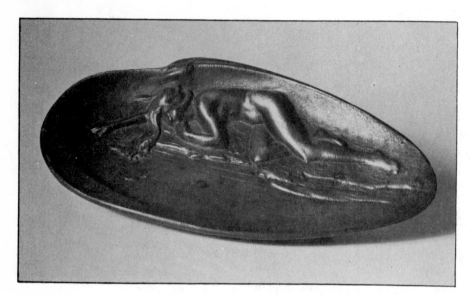

Art Nouveau handled platter;
1905–15; $85–135.

Art Nouveau card tray;
by A. Marionnet; 1890–
1900; $300–450.

Candleholder; 1920–30; $65–85.
Simple but attractive pieces such
as this are still underpriced.

Art Nouveau candle-
holder; 1890–1910; $225–
325. Wonderful detail
greatly enhances the
value of this fine piece.

Art Nouveau candleholder with gold wash; 1890–1900; $600–850. Gold-washed bronze has the weight and appearance of solid gold.

Candelabra; by Tiffany Studios; 1910–15; $850–1,150 the pair.

Candlestick; by Tiffany Studios; 1900–10; $350–425.

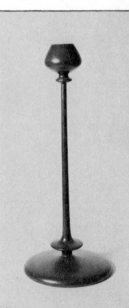

Desk set; 1890–1900; $550–750. Desk sets were among the most popular of Art Nouveau bronze ware.

Desk fixtures; 1920–35. *Left:* Double inkwell; $95–125. *Center:* Stamp box; $65–90. *Right:* Inkwell; $125–175.

Inkwell; 1920–25; $165–245.

Inkwell in the shape of a gondola;
1900–10; $85–115.

Inkwell decorated with beetles in
relief; by Tiffany Studios; 1900–02;
$2,500–3,200. So-called scarab
inkwells are rare and valuable.

Art Nouveau inkstand; 1890–1900;
$130–175.

Inkwell in the form of a chicken; 1900–
10; $175–225.

Top: Inkwell; by Tiffany Studios; 1905–15; $275–350. *Bottom:* Letter opener with handle in the form of a buffalo; 1905–15; $150–200.

Set of blotter ends; 1880–1900; $200–275.

Sealing-wax seals. *Left:* Art Nouveau head; 1890–1900; $120–155. *Center:* Abstract form; 1890–1900; $65–95. *Right:* Art Deco head; 1920–25; $125–160.

Paperweight in the form of a hand; 1910–15; $125–160.

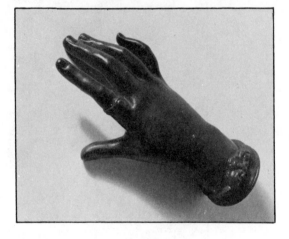

Paperweight in the form of an African woman with a brass necklace; 1935–40; $35–50.

Pair of Art Deco bookends; 1920–30; $85–135.

Pair of bookends, Dante and Beatrice; cast by Pompeian Bronze Works; 1920–30; $185–245.

Pair of Arts and Crafts bookends; by Bradley & Hubbard; 1925–30; $75–125.

Art Nouveau match holder; 1880–1900; $115–155. Usually, the earlier the Art Nouveau figure, the more modestly she is dressed.

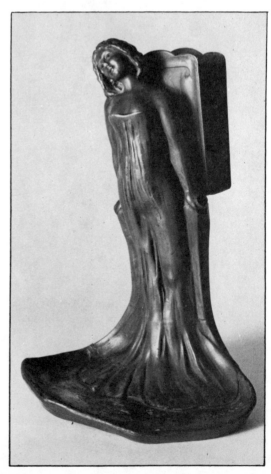

Match holder; 1920–30;
$65–95.

Standing ashtray; 1920–
30; $225–300.

Match holder for wooden
matches; by William
Bernard; New York, N.Y.;
1890–1900; $35–50.

Standing ashtray; 1930–
40; $165–225.

Left and *right:* Pair of
finials; 1890–95; $75–110.
Center: Ice tongs; 1940–
50; $25–55.

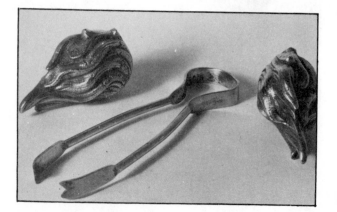

Eagle flagpole finial; 1910–20; $75–115.

Doorknocker; 1910–20; $115–145. An attractive adaptation of a traditional European model.

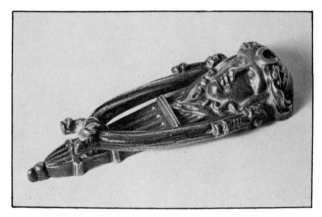

Doorstop in the shape of a sailing ship; 1915–25; $55–75.

Thermometer stand with electro-plated silver finial; 1900–05; $150–185.

Tie rack supported by a pair of dolphins; 1910–20; $60–85.

Beakers; 1900–10. *Left:* $50–65. *Right:*
$60–85.

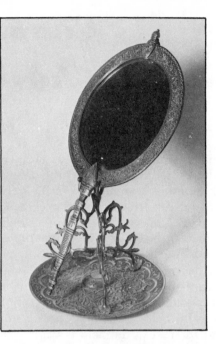

Mirror and mirror rest;
1910–20; $165–245. It is
unusual to find a mirror
of this sort complete with
matching stand.

Brass and bronze tableware in
the Japanese manner; 1920–30.
Left: Covered jar; $90–135.
Center: Plate; $50–70. *Right:*
Vase; $65–90.

Coca-Cola bottle opener;
1935–45; $15–25.

Lamp base with decorative glass
shade; by the Handel Manufacturing Co.; 1900–10; $1,000–
1,400. Some Handel lamps bring
nearly as much as comparable
Tiffany lights.

Country Store Advertiques

The nostalgia for a simpler, better way of life that has swept the United States during the past decade is nowhere more evident than in the field of country store and advertising collectibles. It's not unusual today for collectors to pay thousands of dollars for nineteenth-century trade signs or large, well-preserved Interprise coffee mills. Some collectors have decorated the walls of their homes with lithographed advertising posters—framed like art prints—and others have set up complete country stores in their basements. There is no indication that interest in the field is waning, and enthusiasm and prices continue to grow.

Most collectors are interested in both country store collectibles and advertising collectibles, and frequently there is little or no difference between the two areas. Indeed, few manufacturers could resist employing a useful item—a string holder or ashtray—as an advertising medium. However, the field can be divided into two categories: those objects—such as signs, posters, and trade cards—that were originally intended primarily or exclusively to advertise a product or shop, and those objects—such as coffee mills, flour and coffee bins, and various gum and candy machines—that were necessary to the functioning of the typical late-nineteenth– early-twentieth-century grocery or dry goods store.

One possible reason for the great popularity of these so-called advertiques is the fact that advertising is still a vital part of our society. With many other kinds of antiques, both the object and the function that it once performed are now obsolete. But the techniques employed in advertising have changed little since the nineteenth century, and posters, free samples, and mass advertising remain as much in use today as they were one hundred years ago.

One of the most widely collected advertiques is the advertising poster. These first appeared in the late eighteenth century, as black-and-white woodcuts. The introduction of lithography, in the mid-1800s, soon led to a proliferation of brightly colored tin and paper posters.

Advertising posters have always been regarded as an art form (it is evident from the many existing well-preserved examples dating from the 1880s that even then they were collected for their pictorial qualities). They were often designed by leading lithographers, such as the well-known firm of Currier & Ives.

Most posters were made of paper or cardboard and were intended to be pasted or tacked to a wall or to fit into a wooden frame on the wall of a trolley. Some, however, were made of tin and were designed for permanency. These latter were often used as exterior or interior shop signs. The famous Coca-Cola signs of the period from 1920 to 1940 provide an excellent example.

Though most posters were printed, a few were painted on tin or glass. Perhaps the rarest and most interesting of these are the reverse-glass painted examples, such as the Beech-Nut Fruit Drops signs of the 1930s. Because of their fragility, few of these signs were made, and fewer have survived.

Another category of "pure" advertising memorabilia is trade cards, tiny two- by three-inch lithographed cardboard cards that were handed out on the street (usually by the small boys characteristically referred to as "urchins" in Victorian literature). These cards either urged the passerby to purchase a certain product, such as a cologne or patent medicine, or directed him or her to a specific store. Trade cards were produced in much the same way as advertising posters, and are, in a sense, miniature versions of the posters. Since they come in a vast variety and are quite inexpensive, they represent one of the best areas for collecting and investment in the advertising field.

Once drawn into the store (whether by a tin advertising poster or a card thrust into his or her palm), the customer was offered a variety of products and devices that—aside from rivaling the array of items found in a modern department store—supplies a vast range of potential collectibles to today's collectors.

Every grocery store had one or more coffee mills wherein the roasted beans were ground to order. These great wheeled crushers stood as high as four feet and were usually hand painted in bright colors, such as red and gold. Similar specimens in iron or tin were sold for home use, and quite frequently these bore not only the name of the manufacturer but a coffee producer's advertising as well.

For the children there was an array of gum, nut, and candy machines. Such names as Baby Grand and Delicious still recall for many people the days when penny candy cost just a penny. Though hardly common, twentieth-century dispensing machines of this sort are available today at reasonable prices.

As late as the Second World War, many commodities, such as flour, coffee, and tea, were sold in bulk, and every store had to have a variety of serviceable containers. Most popular among these today are the sturdy oak cabinets in which Diamond dyes were displayed and the many different tin containers that held coffee or tea. The latter frequently have remarkable lithographed tin decoration, featuring everything from American warships to exotic oriental locales.

There were many other dispensers: wooden boxes that held dry biscuits, with colorful lithographed paper labels; glass jars with tightly fitting covers for the storage of everything from peanuts to Borden's Malted Milk; and large round cardboard containers for bulk spices.

All these objects—like nearly everything else in the store—bore some sort of advertiser's message. The blackboard or the adjustable sign that recorded the daily butter and egg prices invariably was furnished by a wholesaler, as were the string dispenser, the cigar cutter, the match safes, the calendars, and even the thermometer. There are so many different examples in each of these categories that it is not unusual to find collectors concentrating on one or more to the exclusion of all other advertiques.

Particularly popular today are serving and tip trays and pocket mirrors. The former, made of lithographed tin, were used in taverns and at soda fountains to serve beverages and make change. Ranging in size from three to sixteen inches in diameter, they are sought for their fine graphics and sentimental renditions of popular scenes. Examples extolling the virtues of Coca-Cola are especially popular and will frequently bring prices in the hundreds of dollars.

The tiny tin-and-glass mirrors were just right for the purse or pocket—and, of course, they too carried an advertiser's message. Given away like trade cards, they frequently promoted hair or beauty care items, bearing on their reverse sides the likenesses of famous movie stars or actresses of the day.

While not, perhaps, as common as tin or paper items, pottery advertising memorabilia is available. Stoneware mugs often bear the name of a brewery or a nonalcoholic beverage like Hires Rootbeer, and it is possible to obtain whole sets of earthenware dishes extolling the virtues of Buster Brown shoes. Especially desirable are topical items, such as the Cream of Wheat cereal bowls that feature a representation of the famous train known as the Twentieth Century Limited.

Not all advertising items are easy to find. Certain objects, either because they were fragile or because they were made in limited numbers, have virtually disappeared. Among the most expensive of all advertiques are certain scarce advertising posters, but other one-of-a-kind items will also bring high prices. The cutout lithographed tin counter sign known as the Jolly Washerwoman is one of these. Only a single example is known to exist, and it is valued at over a thousand dollars. Advertising dolls, such as the Uneeda Biscuit Boy, may bring equally impressive prices when they make their rare appearances on the market.

Perhaps the most exciting thing about the advertising and country store field is that it is (in keeping with the American economy that it mirrors) constantly expanding. It was not so long ago that most people collected only pre-1920s items. Today, the many attractive advertiques of the 1930s, 1940s, and even 1950s are being sought. Moreover, items such as lithographed tins, cardboard boxes, and even paper seed packets are attracting more and more attention. Since many of these items can still be purchased reasonably, the field remains open to the young and less affluent collector.

It should be kept in mind, however, that no area of collecting is as concerned with condition as is advertiques. Advertising collectors are seldom interested in rusted tin or water-stained paper goods. They want their collectibles to be as close to mint condition as possible. Therefore, if one is buying with investment in mind, damaged "bargains" should be avoided. They will seldom appreciate in value.

Reproductions, with the exception of some tins and advertising posters, are uncommon in the field. Furthermore, the reproductions that do exist are obvious to all but the rankest beginner, a pleasant—and unfortunately somewhat rare—situation in the world of antiques.

Lithographed paper advertising poster for the Boston Rubber Shoe Co.; ca. 1900; $135–175.

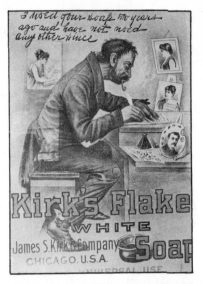

Lithographed paper advertising sign for Kirk's Flake Soap; 1880–90; $400–600. This sign is an extremely rare example of an early advertising poster.

Lithographed paper advertising post for Knox Gelatine; ca. 1920; $85–140 This poster was intended for display a trolley car.

Lithographed cardboard advertising poster; 1890–1900; $350–500. This rare poster was intended to promote the mill at Wahoo, Nebraska.

Lithographed cardboard advertising sign for Arbuckles' Ariosa Coffee; ca. 1893; $400–550.

Lithographed cardboard advertising poster for J. M. Doud and Co.; 1900–10; $350–450. One of the many posters to utilize children as attention getters.

Lithographed paper advertising poster; 1910–15; $65–85. Posters such as this were made with blank spaces for advertisers' names. They would then be printed to order.

Lithographed paper advertising sign for the Northwestern Yeast Co.; 1920–25; $90–130.

Lithographed tin advertising sign for Lipton's Cocoa; 1920–30; $80–125. This sign shows evidence of modern advertising techniques.

Lithographed cardboard trade cards; ca. 1890; $4–7 each. *Left:* Glenn's Sulphur Soap. *Center:* Radway's Ready Relief (a pain killer.) *Right:* Hoyt's German Cologne.

Lithographed paper advertising poster and duplicate cardboard trade card for Eagle Brand Condensed Milk; ca. 1899. Poster; $225–275. Trade card; $5–8.

155

Lithographed tin advertising sign for Royal Baking Powder; ca. 1920; $115–155. Incorporates adjustable butter and egg prices.

Lithographed paper advertising poster for the Metropolitan Life Insurance Co.; 1898; $80–125. Incorporates a calendar. Calendars were among the most popular advertising giveaways.

Lithographed cardboard advertising poster for the Stillman Bottling Co.; 1915; $30–45. Includes a calendar and cutouts. A smaller and less expensive calendar of the sort often available to collectors.

Lithographed paper advertising calendar, one of a set of four produced to promote Buster Brown Shoes; 1906; $250–325 the set.

Lithographed tin advertising sign for Whistle soda pop; 1920–30; $125–175.

Lithographed tin advertising sign for Old Fashion root beer; 1930–35; $75–105.

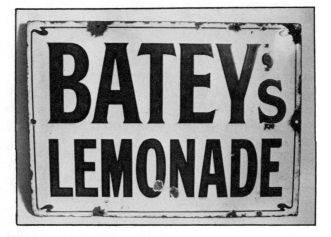

Lithographed tin advertising sign for Batey's Lemonade; 1930–40; $50–70. Tin signs of this sort were usually hung outside a shop.

Advertising sign in gold leaf on red glass background; ca. 1940; $75–125. This sign directed people to the hosiery department in the nationwide chain of Woolworth stores.

Lithographed paper poster indicating registration of a store under the National Recovery Act; 1934; $55–75. These posters were common throughout the United States during the 1930s.

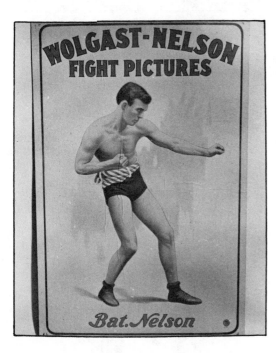

Lithographed paper poster advertising motion pictures of a championship boxing match; 1920–30; $155–195. Posters promoting sporting events were common.

Reverse-glass advertising sign for Buster Brown Shoes; 1920–30; $165–235. This sign is in far better condition than most glass signs.

Reverse-glass advertising sign for Beech-Nut Fruit Drops; 1930–35; $100–165.

Lithographed tin advertising cutout for D. S. Brown & Co.; 1880–90; $1,000–1,400. The Jolly Washerwoman—the only example known. This counter-top promotional device is the top of the line in advertiques.

Lithographed paper advertising fans; 1920–30. *Left to right:* $10–20; $10–15; $8–13. Because of their fragile nature, advertising fans are relatively uncommon, but they remain inexpensive and a good buy.

Lithographed tin string dispenser advertising Swift's Pride Soap; ca. 1908; $1,300–1,850. Another one-of-a-kind advertique, this example is in excellent condition.

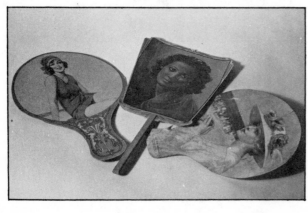

Lithographed tin match safe advertising Buster Brown Bread; 1900–05 $235–285.

158

Photograph-on-glass advertising thermometer; 1930–40; $20–35.

Thermometer advertising Wool Soap; 1925–35; $30–50. Thermometers are of little interest to most collectors because they are usually not very colorful.

Lithographed tin tip tray for Coca-Cola; 1910–20; $90–130. Coca-Cola collectibles are particularly popular.

Lithographed tin tip trays; 1900–20. *Top:* Baker's Cocoa; $65–95. *Center:* Dorne's Carnation Chewing Gum; $25–40. *Bottom:* Fairy Soap; $40–45.

Lithographed cardboard washing-powder boxes; 1920–35. *Left:* Grandma's; $15–22. *Center:* Fun-to-Wash; $20–35. *Right:* Gold Dust; $10–25. An underpriced area of advertiques.

Lithographed tin and cardboard cleanser and starch containers. *Left:* Chic; ca. 1925; $15–20. *Center left:* Polly Prim; 1920–30; $10–15. *Center right:* Wyandotte; 1930–35; $25–32. *Right:* Electric Lustre Starch; ca. 1883; $15–24.

Lithographed tin talcum powder tins; 1900–10. *Left:* Perfumed Violet; $50–60. *Center:* Pompeia; $35–40. *Right:* Yankee; $125–150. The Yankee container is the only known example.

Glass bottles in the Art Deco style with lithographed paper labels; 1925–35. *Left:* Brilliantine; $5–8. *Center:* Carminade; $15–22. *Right:* Lily of the Valley; $10–17.

Lithographed tin coffee containers; 1910–20. *Left:* Bunker Hill; $40–55. *Center top:* Kamargo; $60–85. *Center bottom:* Gillies; $45–65. *Right:* Rose Bud; $20–35. Rose Bud has a paper label.

Lithographed tin storage bin for pepper; 1900–10; $100–135.

oden storage and shipping box with
ographed paper labels for Austin &
aves Biscuit; ca. 1900; $65–85.

Wooden shipping barrel
with lithographed paper
label for Keystone Mince
Meat; 1920–25; $45–60.
Barrels of this sort are
seldom found intact.

Beauty aid containers; 1925–35. *Left:*
Lithographed cardboard box for Three
Flowers Vanishing Cream; $7–15.
Center: Lithographed tin for Three
Flowers Face Powder; $15–24. *Right:*
Lithographed cardboard box for Hair
Youth; $9–16.

Lithographed tin cookie
box with a portrait of the
actress Gloria Swanson
as an Indian maiden;
1930–35; $45–65. This
cover was designed by the
famous illustrator Henry
Clive.

Pressed-glass storage jar for National
Biscuit Co.; 1915–20; $70–85, An
attractive and well-formed collectible.

Glass and enameled-steel penny peanut machine; by Northwestern Co.; Morris, Ill.; 1925–35; $85–135.

Oak and cast-iron Baby Grand penny bubble-gum machine; 1930–40; $110–145. Candy and gum machines are fast becoming prime collectibles.

Lithographed metal penny chewing gum machine; 1935–40; $90–130.

Lithographed tin and steel dispenser for Sweet Chocolate; by National Automatic Vending Machine Co.; Philadelphia, Pa.; 1930–40; $70–90.

Glass, oak, and lithographed tin storage container for Mansfield's Pepsin Gum; 1885–90; $185–255.

Uneeda Biscuit Boy advertising doll, bisque head in yellow coat with black composition boots; 1915–20; $750–950. Lithographed paper poster for N.B.C. (National Biscuit Co.) products; 1920–30; $80–135. Advertising dolls are rare and in great demand.

ZU ZU Ginger Snaps advertising dolls; ca. 1915; $135–200 each. ZU ZU lithographed paper advertising poster; 1920–30; $80–125.

Lithographed steel toy delivery truck advertising Tag Soap; 1915–25; $75–105. This was probably intended as a giveaway. Lithographed Tag soap wrapper with original bar of soap; 1915–25; $2–5.

Lithographed tin candy containers; dated 1914; $25–40 each.

Household Accessories

While many antiques enthusiasts devote themselves to the lovely—and expensive—silver, art glass, pottery, and bronze produced during the past century, there is a growing army of collectors that is interested in the less-expensive everyday objects that reflect the life-styles of past decades. For many of these collectors this is a quest for identity; many of the wood, brass, and textile objects that they seek are things that they recall from the homes of their parents or grandparents.

Most of these household collectibles are anonymous—few manufacturers thought them important enough to mark. However, most of us are more likely to recognize a Ronson lighter than a piece of Galle glass. There were more of the former, and they were available to a much wider cross section of the American people.

Collectors of household items have thousands of objects to choose from from every room of the house. They can start in the kitchen with hand-stitched pot holders; a pair of Bakelite salt and pepper shakers in the form of Trylon and Perisphere, made famous by the World's Fair of 1939; or some of the black memorabilia, such as wooden towel racks and napkin holders. Or they can join the growing number of enthusiasts for the chrome-plated wares produced during the 1930s by the Chase Manufacturing Company. Chase wares—which include complete tea sets, a variety of folding trays and serving dishes, as well as electric coffee urns—are in the best Art Deco mode and are at present an excellent investment. Much the same can be said for the relatively uncommon early aluminum wares. Aluminum was long believed to be poisonous, and pre-1910 aluminum cooking utensils are rare.

A large number of collectible items come from the living room and dining area. Most of them reflect the changing tastes and expanding horizons of Americans during the late nineteenth and early twentieth centuries. As smoking, for example, became acceptable in mixed company (it had previously been an all-male pleasure par-taken of in special "smoking rooms"), and as women in larger numbers joined the ranks of smokers, a whole panoply of items was created to serve the new habit. Cigarette boxes in everything from Victorian mother-of-pearl to the chrome and blue glass of the 1920s arrived on the scene.

A profusion of lighters and ashtrays also appeared. Many of the lighters were portable, but there were also permanent lighters, which were meant to have a place among the household furnishings. Ronson pioneered this field, and its figural cigarette lighters, including airplanes and animals, are among the more popular twentieth-century collectibles. Ashtrays, of course, have been with us for a long time. Those of the Art Nouveau period (1870 to 1910) are often decorated with lush nudes, reflecting their use in smoking rooms or men's clubs, for few matrons of the period would have tolerated such things in the living room. But during the swinging 1920s the body as a form for ashtrays reappeared—and in mixed company.

Social drinking also entered a new vogue, accompanied by everything from Chase-manufactured cocktail mixers and serving sets to brass bottle openers and corkscrews.

Brass, in fact, was an extremely important metal during the first half of the twentieth century. Less expensive than bronze, it served not only as a base metal for chrome and silver-plated items but also as a sculptural medium. From Art Nouveau to Art Deco, sculptural pieces were cast in brass and in the ubiquitous silverlike pot metal. Both metals could be plated or left as they were, but in either case they provided an inexpensive medium in which well-known (or not-so-well-known) sculptural examples could be duplicated for sale to those unable to afford the real thing. "Bronzed" Art Nouveau figurines are frequently of considerable artistic merit and warrant real consideration by the collector.

Collectibles may also be found in the library. Most common are bookends, some of which are in the hammered-brass finish made popular by Arts and Crafts movement creators such as Elbert Hubbard. Equally important, though, are inkstands and penholders, both of which are found in large numbers. Made in brass, pot metal, or cast iron, they reflect all the styles of the past century. Though still available in some numbers, these pieces are increasing in value.

A variety of collectibles comes from the bedroom, including boudoir dressing-table sets and many small boxes, some delicately made of lace and cardboard for the preservation of scented handkerchiefs, some made of pewter or pot metal for holding trinkets or cosmetics. All reflect an era during which a woman could spend more time preparing for a party or dinner than attending it.

Even the entrance hall or foyer provides interesting collectibles. There are cast-iron doorstops and hammered-brass umbrella stands as well as the once-important card tray. The Victorians loved to visit, and everyone had a visiting card—giving his name and address—which was always ceremoniously deposited in a small brass or pot-metal tray conveniently left beside the front door. These trays, as well as the mother-of-pearl cases in which the cards were kept, are fascinating survivors of a more elegant time.

Perhaps more than any other area of collectibles, household accessories truly reflect the growth of American society. The farther back in time that the collector goes, the less variety he finds. It is not only that more articles are produced today than were produced in earlier generations. During the 1880s and 1890s, the means of the average citizen were limited. This, combined with a strong, puritanical streak that was opposed to any sort of ostentatious display, prevented an accumulation of household accessories. As the 1900s dawned, the religious strictures became weaker, and the rise of a well-to-do middle class heralded the advent of the so-called consumer economy.

By 1920, the prosperity brought on by the First World War had made it possible for more of the population to own an increasing number of things. During the 1930s, despite the inroads of the depression, the average household included hundreds of items that are now regarded as highly collectible.

Nor has the process come to an end. The plastic and metal accessories of the 1950s and 1960s are already attracting attention, and it is evident that within a few years this era will be regarded as a rich source of collectibles.

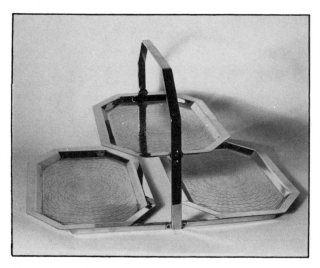

Chrome-plated coffee set; by Chase Manufacturing Co.; 1930–40; $140–190.

Chrome-plated brass serving tray; by Chase Manufacturing Co.; 1930–40; $55–75. Chase was one of the most sophisticated makers of chrome, and its wares are rapidly becoming collector's items.

Brass and copper coffee-pot in the Arts and Crafts mode; 1910–15; $225–275. Brass and copper have long been used in the kitchen and on the table.

Chrome-plated electric coffee urn, tray, sugar bowl, and creamer; 1930–40; $70–100 the set.

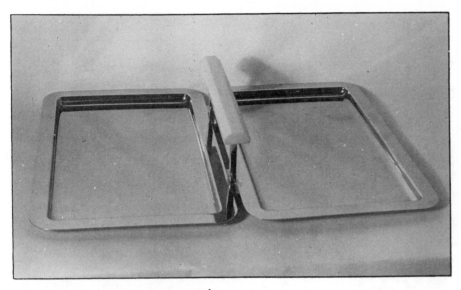

Folding chrome serving tray in metal and Bakelite; by Manning Bowman Manufacturing Co.; 1930–35; $30–40.

Plastic salt and pepper shakers; 1939; $15–20 pair. Designed as souvenirs of the New York World's Fair. Plastic is fast becoming a collectible.

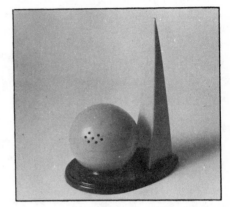

Wooden towel rack; 1935–45; $25–35.

Painted-wood napkin holder; 1935–45; $5–8. Wooden kitchen collectibles are still relatively inexpensive.

Wooden-handled brushes in the forms of black figures; 1930–40; $8–14.

Wooden letter or magazine rack with burned-on decoration (pyrography); 1910–20; $30–45. Hobbyists could purchase pieces like this blank and decorate them themselves.

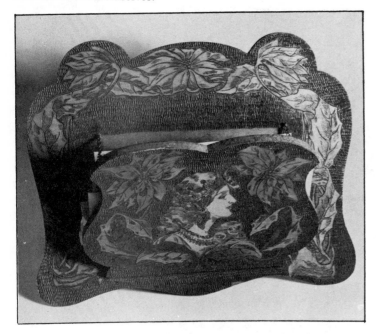

Chrome-plated accessories; 1930–40. *Left front:* Bonbon tray; $13–20. *Left rear:* Desk lamp; $70–100. *Center:* Goblet; $25–30. *Right rear:* Cocktail mixer; $55–70. *Right front:* Lighter; $48–51. *Far right:* Match and cigarette box; $25–29.

Embroidered pot-holder cover and pot holders; 1935–45; $7–15 the set.

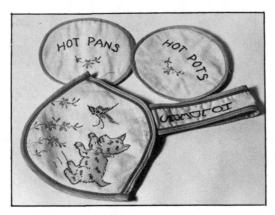

Wooden pot-holder rack; 1940–50; $8–15. A great variety of novelty items for kitchen use were made of wood, and they are now quite collectible.

168

Blue-glass bowl mounted in metal frame; 1900–15; $35–55. Because it was light and inexpensive to produce, pot metal was the basic medium for many housewares of the 1900s.

Extremely rare milk-glass water cooler mounted on an elaborate pot-metal frame; by Simpson, Hall and Miller; Wallingford, Conn.; 1881; $700–950. This is one of two known examples.

Hammered-copper candlestick; by Gustav Stickley; 1910–12; $375–475.

Copper chafing dish on oak base; by Gustav Stickley; 1905–07; $350–475. The fact that this piece was made by a famous furniture designer greatly increases its value.

Hammered-copper umbrella stand; by Gustav Stickley; 1905–09; $900–1,200. A rare and well-designed example of a mundane object.

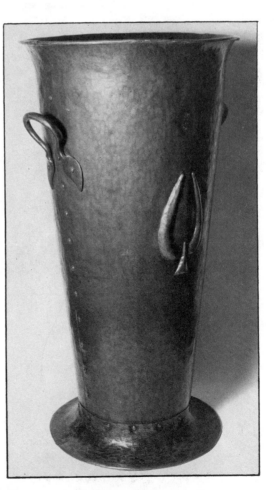

Pair of wrought-iron candleholders with iridescent glass founts;
by Tiffany Studios; 1900–10;
$2,500–2,900. Tiffany wrought
iron is rare and expensive.

Wood-and-brass chamber
candlestick; by Charles Rohlfs;
ca. 1907; $900–1,200.

Pewter candelabra; by Liberty
Manufacturing Co.; 1900–10;
$1,750–2,000. These rare pieces
were designed by Knox and
reflect pewter's traditional role
as "poor man's silver."

Pot-metal and glass electric lamp; by
Nu Art Manufacturing Co.; 1925–30;
$250–310.

Bronzed pot-metal electric banquet
lamp; 1910–15; $220–285. Pot metal
was often stained or plated to make it
look like bronze or brass.

Brass Art Deco table lamp; 1935–40;
$125–165. This lamp is made entirely
of sheet and rod brass.

Pot-metal night-light with multicolored glass; 1935–40; $200–270.

Popsicle-stick table lamp; 1940–50;
$60–80. Popsicle sticks were an
inexpensive hobby material.

Art Deco chrome night-light; 1935–45;
$40–55.

Pair of stainless-steel bookends in the form of greyhounds; by Ronson Art Works; 1925–35; $145–170.

Stainless-steel and Bakelite bookend; by Ronson Art Works; 1930–35; $60–85.

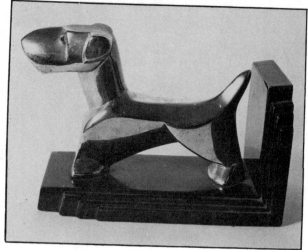

Composition material writing set with letter opener of bone and mother-of-pearl; 1890–1910; $125–155.

Carved-wood inkwell in the form of an owl; 1900–10; $65–95.

Bakelite Art Deco penholder; 1935–40; $15–25.

Copper and brass inkwell set in the Arts and Crafts mode; 1905–15; $80–125.

Multicolored marble penholder in the form of an eagle; 1930–40; $70–100. The carver of this unusual piece has used the color differences in the marble to give the bird a lifelike appearance.

Art Deco chrome lighter and cigarette case; 1935–40; $35–55.

Ceramic and leather smoking set; by
Dunhill Co.; 1925–35; $130–170.

Painted-lead tobacco box; ca. 1890;
$145–185. This large and heavy box
was intended for storage.

Blue-glass cigarette box; 1935–45;
$25–35. Reflective blue glass was a
popular medium in the late 1930s.

Bakelite and chrome cigarette box;
1930–40; $40–60.

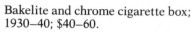

Chrome and plastic cigarette box and
ashtray; 1930–35; $15–25. Easy to
clean, attractive, and durable, chrome
steel was the "poor man's silver" of the
1930s.

Bronze-washed pot-metal and marble standing floor ashtray; 1930–40; $165–245.

Oxidized metal ashtray with brass fixtures; 1925–30; $30–45.

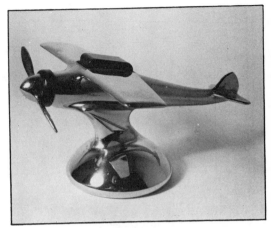

Stainless-steel cigarette lighter in the form of an airplane; 1925–30; $75–105.

Stainless-steel dogs for the smoking room; 1930–40. *Left:* Ashtray; by Haganauer; $65–85. *Right:* Cigarette lighter; $50–65.

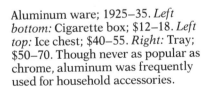

Aluminum ware; 1925–35. *Left bottom:* Cigarette box; $12–18. *Left top:* Ice chest; $40–55. *Right:* Tray; $50–70. Though never as popular as chrome, aluminum was frequently used for household accessories.

Aluminum and painted-glass Art Deco
vanity case; 1930–35; $35–55.

Pewter powder box; 1920–25; $40–60.
An attractive and somewhat uncommon boudoir piece.

Celluloid jewelry box with brown
transfer decoration on cover; 1910–15;
$25–45.

Cardboard handkerchief box covered
with silk chiffon; 1920–30; $25–35.

Copper box in the Arts and Crafts mode; 1905–10; $150–200.

Mother-of-pearl visiting card cases; 1900–10. *Left:* $65–85. *Center:* $80–115. *Right:* $40–50. No proper Victorian could be without his or her visiting cards and card case.

Silvered pot-metal wall plaque; 1925–35; $60–85.

Tin and brass tape measure in the form of a clock; 1925–35; $35–45.

Cast-iron commemorative picture frame; dated 1917; $40–55. Intended for the picture of a boy away at war.

Cast-iron doorstop; 1900–10; $55–70.

Plaster-of-Paris figure, "The Flapper"; 1920–30; $30–45.

Wood and copper model of an airplane; 1935–40; $115–145.

Marble figural group; 1880–90; $135–155. Small mantel decorations of this sort were popular in the late 19th century.

Sheet-brass wall plaque; 1940–50; $15–25.

Pot-metal thermometer with gold wash; 1910–15; $50–75.

Thermometer set in a colored photograph behind glass; 1940–50; $15–22. Thermometers like this were often given away by stores and service companies.

Tortoiseshell lorgnette; 1880–90; $115–135. This pair of long-handled glasses has a completely handcarved handle.

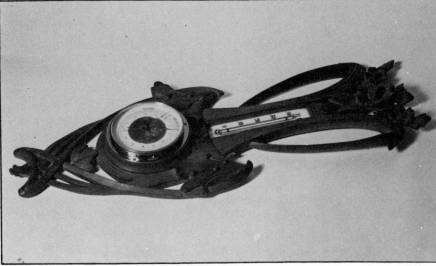

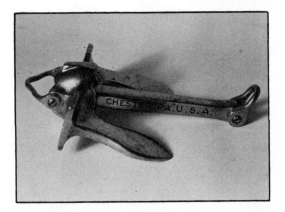

Glass and metal barometer in a carved wood frame; 1880–90; $175–235. Weather predicting devices are becoming a source of serious collector interest.

Stainless-steel miniature anchor; ca. 1896; $65–90. Probably intended for use as a salesman's sample.

Jewelry

Jewelry is a particularly appealing collectible for several reasons: if set in gold or silver or with precious gems, it has intrinsic value; it can be used; and—of prime importance to many collectors—it is so small that a substantial collection can be housed in the smallest apartment.

The collector interested in American jewelry of the period 1880 to 1950 will find a multitude of treasures from which to choose. There is an abundance of late Victorian pieces. Indeed, the last decades of the nineteenth century were a period of great show and opulence, and jewelry was very popular. There were two general types of jewelry: primary jewelry, made of gem-encrusted precious metals and intended for use only on great occasions; and secondary jewelry, which consisted of semiprecious stones set in silver or plate for everyday use.

Both types of jewelry are of importance to the modern collector; the Victorian flair for detail, excellence of workmanship, and ability to create charming small things is evident in nearly every piece regardless of its original value. The variety available is, in part, a result of the fact that among the moneyed classes women had little to do other than display their wealth. It is also attributable to the general custom, among all classes, of giving jewelry as gifts at both joyous occasions and tragic ones.

Victorian jewelry varies greatly in style and is, in fact, a mirror of the many styles—Gothic, Rococo, Renaissance, and so on—popular during the period. Egyptian Revival, for example, appears not only in scarab rings but also in the far more common snake-form rings and bracelets. The curling serpents, often with glaring eyes of ruby or opal, seem to have had a fascination for women of the time. Even Queen Victoria owned a snake bracelet.

There are also, of course, Art Nouveau pieces, some of them made by famous craftsmen like Tiffany and Lalique. These include bracelets, rings, and especially brooches. The motifs are appropriate to the period: long, flowing floral and animal forms done in everything from gold to natural wood.

For the wealthy, gems were de rigueur, and as the century came to an end, diamonds assumed a place of first importance. In the 1880s they were set in heavy flamboyant mountings, but by the 1890s social usage dictated settings of wisps of gold or platinum from which the great gems hung like drops of dew on a blade of grass.

In polite society diamonds were reserved for the married woman; girls and young ladies were limited to such baubles as rubies, pearls, and emeralds. In the 1880s these were usually set in bracelets and brooches because the long hair and high necklines of the period limited use of other jewelry. But at the turn of the century, short hair and low-cut gowns returned, and with them came a plethora of necklaces and earrings. At the same time, silver, which had been somewhat in eclipse, was returned to favor, particularly in the form of heavy carved bracelets in the Indian taste. The Eastern influence is also seen in the dragon motif common to many pieces.

Much of the finer jewelry made after 1900 was made in suites of several matching pieces (pins, bracelets, tiaras) intended to be worn together. Unfortunately, many of these suites have been broken up over the years, making it difficult to obtain a complete set. It is possible, however, to obtain suites in semiprecious stones from the period from 1900 to 1920. It was during this period also that paste or artificial glass became generally available, and, combined with silver-plated settings, it offered an inexpensive alternative for the frugal. Marcasites, tiny gemlike pieces of cut and polished steel, served a similar purpose.

Though relatively unimportant in comparison with the large quantity of Victorian and post-Victorian jewelry, jewelry produced by craftsmen of the Arts and Crafts movement is available. From 1890 until well into the 1920s these studio jewelers created unusual forms employing semiprecious stones, such as garnet and topaz, and massive settings of silver or even copper. Today, such pieces are rather hard to come by.

Following the First World War the so-called modern movement came to the fore, and jewelry design changed greatly in response to the influence of the arts (particularly cubism), the effects of mass production, and the introduction of new materials, such as plastics and chrome. The forms of jewelry, which had traditionally been based on natural sources, became angular and geometric. During the 1920s this hard line was softened by an almost playful experimentation, but with the coming of the Great Depression, a severity of form set in, a formalism that was in sharp contrast to the pastels that dominated the color scheme.

The trademark of this period was the string of beads, and amazingly long ropes of cut-glass or rock beads adorned the flappers of the 1920s and early 1930s. Other materials used in jewelry production included amber (or its plastic substitute); ivory; black onyx; jade (in large, flat, relief-carved ring stones); tortoiseshell (for belt buckles and hatpins); a whole variety of attractive stones, ranging from granite to rose quartz; and even colored sealing wax. There was also a great deal of enameled jewelry during the Art Deco period. There had been enameled jewelry during the Victorian period, of course, but enamelware became an art form during the 1930s.

Still, Art Deco jewelry does not compare in either quantity or quality with that of the late Victorian era. During the 1920s and 1930s, women, the major wearers of jewelry, were too active to use the great quantities allocated to women of the Victorian age. Moreover, the economic decline of the 1930s made the wearing of lavish adornment both prohibitively expensive and almost immoral (to all but the most insensitive). As a consequence, jewelry of the 1920s and 1930s is for the most part confined to rings, pins, and necklaces. The elaborate pieces so popular during the earlier era are gone.

During the 1940s and 1950s the boom in costume jewelry, which had been developed just before the Second World War, continued, and great quantities of rather grotesque jewelry made of pot metal, plastic, and painted wood flooded the market. Some of these items are now considered collectible, though their value is more nostalgic than aesthetic.

One should not overlook men's jewelry. Rings have been with us for a long time, and in former times there were also lavish buttons and hair buckles. Contemporary men's jewelry is more mundane. Watch fobs, usually made of silver or gold, abound. There are also such oddments as cigar cutters, bill and coin holders, and fraternal jewelry. Pocketknives can form a whole collection, as can cuff links. Although some of these items were adorned with gemstones, men's jewelry was for the most part severe in line and decoration.

Since there is so much of it to choose from, collecting jewelry can be confusing. It is very much a matter of taste and pocketbook. Buy what you like, but look for good workmanship, pleasing design, and soundness of materials. If these qualities are present, the absence of gold or gems will matter little—without these qualities, precious materials are of little help.

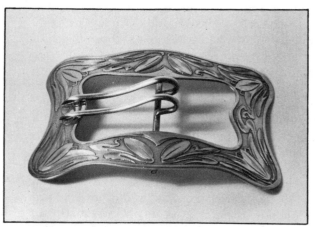

Sterling silver Art Nouveau belt buckle; 1880–90; $60–75.

Sterling silver Art Nouveau belt; 1900–10; $1,200–1,500. Elaborately crafted silver belts are rare and expensive.

Left: Enamel and silver Art Deco belt buckle; 1925–35; $75–115. *Right:* Silver Art Nouveau belt buckle; by Shiebler; 1890–1900; $115–145.

Electroplated silver belt buckle with Indian-head motif; 1900–10; $20–30.

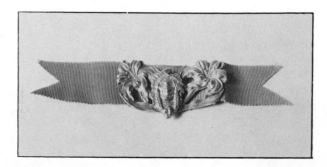

Art Deco belt buckle of artificial diamonds and rubies set in a pot-metal mounting; 1930–40; $12–18.

Sterling silver coin bracelet; 1889–90;
$135–165.

Sterling silver bracelet; by Shiebler
Silver Company; 1890–1900; $95–125.
Shows Eastern influence.

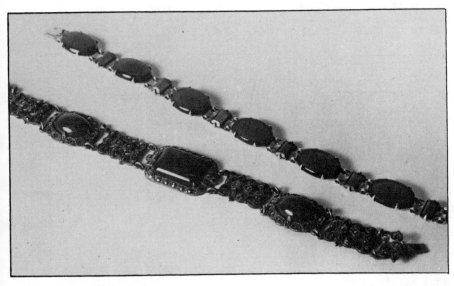

Art Deco bracelets; 1925–35. *Left:*
Silver with marcasites and onyx;
$115–150. *Right:* Silver and onyx;
$75–100.

Sterling silver bracelet set with
diamonds; 1920–30; $1,400–1,700.

183

Sterling silver bracelet; 1910–20; $75–115. Horseback-riding motif.

Sterling silver and enamel snake bracelet with seed pearls; 1890–1900; $145–185.

Bakelite bracelet; 1930–40; $25–35. Bakelite was a popular material for inexpensive jewelry during the 1930s.

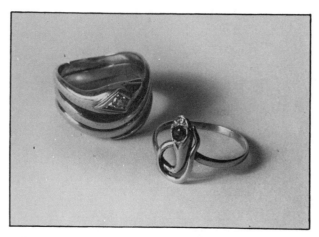

Gold snake rings; 1880–1900. *Left:* With diamond; $350–500. *Right:* With ruby; $175–245.

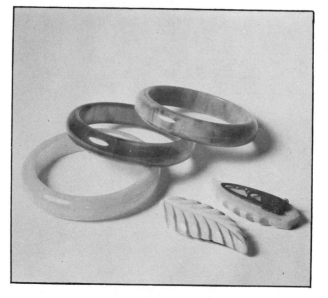

Left: Bakelite bracelets; 1930–40; $35–50. *Right:* Pair of Bakelite hair clips; 1930–40; $20–30.

Left: Gold ring with small rubies; 1930–40; $200–250. *Right:* Silver ring with diamond chips; $125–165.

Silver and marcasite ring; 1930–40; $70–100.

Gold Art Nouveau ring; 1890–1900; $350–475. The excellent work and detail make this an outstanding ring.

Gold rings; 1910–20. *Left:* With garnet and opals; $150–200. *Right:* With garnet and sapphires; $180–260.

Gold and cut stone ring; 1915–25; $100–165.

Necklace of carved rose quartz; 1920–30; $155–205.

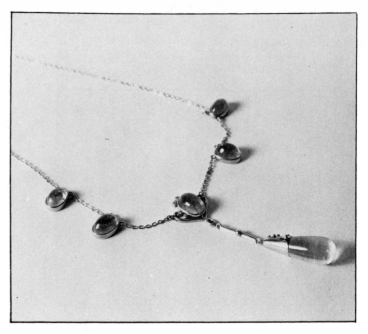

Necklace of sterling silver and enamel with mother-of-pearl drop; 1900–10; $300–375. The naturalistic forms of the Art Nouveau period lend themselves to necklace and pendant construction.

Gold and pink tourmaline necklace; 1900–10; $175–250.

Left: Sterling silver pendant with enamel center; 1900–10; $65–95. *Right:* Sterling silver, enamel, and colored glass necklace with glass drop; 1910–20; $300–400.

Carved ivory pendant; 1920–30; $185–235.

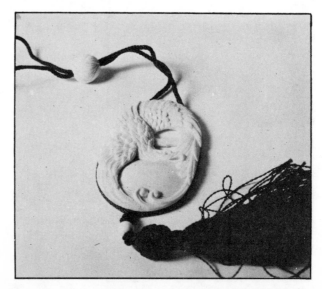

Pendant in black onyx with gold-washed sterling silver mounting; 1930–40; $145–190.

Art Nouveau figural pendants; 1890–1900. *Left:* Gold-washed sterling silver; signed Bryk; $145–185. *Right:* Sterling silver; $115–160.

Left: Sterling silver and enamel pendant; by Charles Horner; 1900–10; $265–345. *Right:* Sterling silver brooch with turquoise; 1925–35; $65–90.

Left: Sterling silver and enamel pin; 1910–20; $125–150. *Center:* Sterling silver and enamel pendant; by Charles Horner; 1900–10; $325–350. *Right:* Sterling silver and enamel pin; by Charles Horner; 1900–20; $110–125.

Sterling silver and enamel necklace; 1920–30; $135–175. Art Deco necklaces and pendants are as popular today as they were in the 1920s and 1930s.

187

Sterling silver and enamel Art Deco pendants; 1930–40. *Top:* $45–65. *Center:* $70–95. *Bottom:* $85–115.

Sterling silver and enamel Art Deco pendants; 1930–40. *Left:* $60–85. *Center:* $75–100. *Right:* $55–75.

Sterling silver and enamel Art Deco necklace; 1930–40; $125–170.

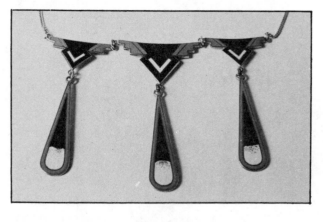

Sterling silver and enamel necklace; 1935–45; $95–145.

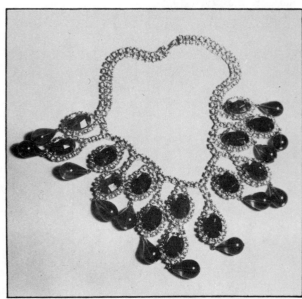

Necklace of gem cut glass mounted on pot metal; 1940–50; $35–55.

Brooch of carved pink coral; 1880–1900; $90–120. In the Italian manner.

Silver and gold Arts and Crafts brooch; 1890–1900; $175–245.

Sterling silver Art Nouveau brooches; 1885–95. *Left:* $45–60. *Right:* $55–85.

Brooches; by Georg Jensen; 1930–45. *Center left:* Floral; $135–165. *Center right:* Bird; $125–155. *Top:* Floral with onyx; $160–225. *Bottom:* Openwork; $105–135.

Gold and enamel Arts and Crafts pin; 1900–10; $155–205. Animal and floral motifs were preferred by the craftsmen of the Arts and Crafts movement.

189

Sterling silver Art Nouveau brooch;
1880–1900; $55–80.

Left: Sterling silver Egyptian Revival
pin in gold wash; 1930–40; $25–35.
Center: Sterling silver dragonflies with
turquoise; 1900–10; $85–125. *Right:*
Sterling silver and enamel beetle; by
Charles Horner; 1900–10; $75–115.

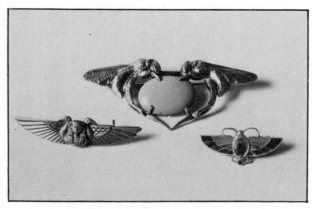

Satsuma porcelain enamel brooch;
Japan; 1920–30; $125–175.

Sterling silver and translucent enamel
pin; 1920–30; $110–145.

Sterling silver dog pins;
1890–1930; $40–64 each.

Brooch of pot metal, rhinestones, and enamel; 1930–40; $20–30.

Brooch and matching earrings of pot metal and rhinestones; 1940–50; $25–35 the set.

Plastic Mickey Mouse pins; 1950–60; $15–20 each.

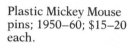

Pair of sterling silver earrings; 1920–30; $20–35.

Sterling silver and enamel brooch and matching earrings; 1930–40; $65–85.

Plastic earrings; 1940–50; $8–15 the pair.

Earrings of painted wood; 1940–50; $3–6 the pair.

Pair of cuff links in jet; 1920–30; $15–22.

Cuff links of the snap-apart variety in silver metal and plastic; 1930–40; $10–15 the pair.

Left: Rosary of carved wood; 1900–15; $85–125. *Right:* Pencil in the form of a cross; 1900–15; $50–70. Both pieces are novelties of the type called stanhopes. They have a small viewing hole through which a tiny picture can be seen.

Sterling silver men's jewelry; 1910–30.
Left bottom: Cigar cutter; $35–50. *Left
top:* Pair of cuff links; $28–45. *Center:*
Enameled stickpin; $30–45. *Right:*
Money clip; $25–40.

Sterling silver charms given away at
fraternal meetings; 1930–40; $35–60
each.

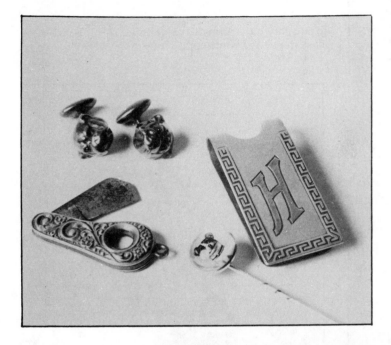

Gold stickpins; 1900–10. *Left:* 50–70.
Right: $40–60.

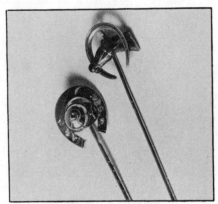

Brass pendant in the form of a small
book filled with tiny pictures; dated
1929; $45–60.

Gold Art Nouveau watch
pin; 1900–10; $70–85. In
the days before wrist-
watches, women pinned
their watches to their
blouses or coats with pins
like this.

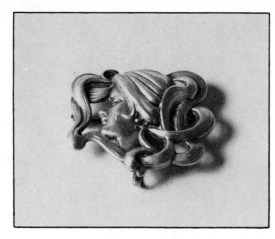

Sterling silver Art Nouveau watch pin;
1890–1900; $100–135.

Watch fob in the form of a miniature
flask in red and white gold; 1880–
1900; $185–225.

Sterling silver perfume flask; 1910–20;
$30–45.

Sterling silver Art
Nouveau woman's purse;
Germany; 1890–1910;
$85–125.

Compact case of brass, Bakelite, and glass; 1925–35; $30–45.

Compact case of brass, Bakelite, and glass; 1930–40; $35–45.

Pair of sterling silver and enamel shoe buckles; 1920–25; $40–55.

Sterling silver key ring in the form of a belt; 1920–30; $30–45.

Pair of shoe buckles in cut steel and glass beads; 1920–30; $15–22.

195

Cameras

Although cameras have been around since 1839, there were no real collectors or collections of photographic materials before the 1900s. In fact, before Eastman Kodak's purchase of the Parisian Gabriel Cromer's collection in 1939, there was no major photographic collection in the United States. The Cromer collection became the nucleus of the famous International Museum of Photography at Rochester, New York, and its acquisition greatly stimulated American interest in photographic collectibles. Today, there are thousands of collectors of photographic "hardware" (cameras and projectors) and ephemera (advertisements, manuals, and books), and there are more than twenty collector clubs.

Today's collectors have a wide field from which to choose. Thousands of cameras were made between 1839—the year in which Louis Daguerre marketed the first daguerreotype—and the present time. Some types, of course, are rare and hard to obtain at any price, but most are abundant and inexpensive.

While some collectors specialize with a given type of camera or concentrate on a single manufacturer, such as Eastman Kodak or Leica, most seek a broad range of products. The bulk of the acquisitions of such collectors fall within one of three categories: box, folding, or 35mm. In each of these divisions the majority of the machines found are either studio models, used by professionals, or the more common hobby or general purpose devices sold to the general public. There are, however, a limited number of other cameras that served unusual purposes, such as detective cameras, often designed to look like books or handbags; miniature cameras, such as the famous Minox; panoramic cameras for photographing landscapes or large crowds; and the stereo cameras used to produce the stereoscopic cards that were so popular in the period from 1880 to 1910.

The first photographic devices were plate cameras: the image was taken on a metal or glass plate and was one of a kind. There was no negative. Between 1839 and the middle of the nineteenth century several kinds of plate cameras were developed. However, by the beginning of the period in which we are interested (1880 to 1950) only one type continued in use—the tintype camera, which was commonly used, even in the 1930s, by itinerant or street photographers. These cameras were wood framed, with leather bellowslike bodies that could be moved back and forth on a track to focus the picture. Although many of these cameras are a century old, they are usually inexpensive because of the large number still available.

Most collectors concentrate on paper-film cameras, the first of which was made in 1887 by George Eastman. Eastman's invention revolutionized photography and enabled him to found a photographic empire. Before Eastman, photography—because of the complex processes required to shoot pictures and, particularly, to develop the film—was primarily a field for professionals. Eastman changed all that by designing a simple, inexpensive (by 1901 his Kodak Brownie was selling for twenty-five cents!) instrument and doing the developing himself. His slogan, "You press the button, we do the rest," told it all. The novice photographer bought the film and camera, loaded up, took his pictures, and sent the exposed film to the Kodak factory. It came back fully developed. To us this seems ordinary, but at the time it was revolutionary.

Eastman Kodak dominated the camera field for generations and produced dozens of different photographic devices. Most clearly associated with his name, though, is the box camera, a square or rectangular camera made of wood, metal, leather, or, after 1930, plastic. Eastman box cameras are usually one of the novice collector's first acquisitions, and among the most popular of these are the Brownie and the Senior and Junior Pocket Kodaks.

The success of the box camera did not keep Eastman from looking to the future, and in 1890 he marketed a folding Kodak. Folding cameras had been around for some time—they were developed in response to the need for a compact, easily transported photographic device—but Eastman's was the first efficient and inexpensive model. Among the many Eastman folding cameras, two are in great demand with modern collectors. These are the Autographics, which produced postcard-sized shots at a time when postcards were extremely popular, and the Art Deco-style Bantam of the 1930s.

Such American models notwithstanding, many collectors also seek out the many fine European cameras. Among these, Leicas are the favorites. The development of the 35mm camera is associated with this firm. Following the organization of the movie industry in the early 1900s, large quantities of 35mm movie film became available. It was not long before still-camera manufacturers decided to take advantage of this situation. Oaskar Barnade, who was employed at the Leitz Optical Works in Wetzler, Germany, designed a metal-cased 35mm camera in 1912, and by 1925 it was being sold commercially. Though four other 35mm cameras were patented between 1912 and 1915 (including the American-made Simplex and Tourist models), Leica dominated the field. Indeed, one measure of Leica's impor-tance is the large number of pirated Leica reproductions (including Russian and Japanese models).

There are many attractive American 35mm cameras, including types produced both in the 1930s and after the conclusion of the Second World War. Among the more attractive of these collector's items are the Memo, made by the Ansco Company of Binghamton, New York, and the Agfa Speedex, which dates to the 1940s.

Movie cameras are considered highly collectible, though the variety available is considerably less than the variety of still cameras. Eastman Kodak was a pioneer in this field, too, and its 16 mm Cine Kodak was long a popular home-movie camera. Other names to look for are Keystone, Briskin, and Pathé.

Various Polaroid-type cameras are also collectible. These developed from the "street" cameras of the early 1900s which were used by penny photographers and incorporated a developing tank attached to the camera tripod. Though primarily a postwar phenomenon, modern Polaroids are already attracting collector attention.

There are few areas of collectibles in which the range of appealing objects is as great or the opportunity for assembling a collection at modest prices as good as in the field of cameras. Some acquisitions can also be used—another advantage.

Bellows-type wooden camera. the Eastman View Finder; by Eastman Kodak; 1881–85; $185–235. Good condition and famous name enhance the value of this camera.

Bellows-type wooden folding camera by American Optica Co.; 1880–90; $7. 105. Lack of the devalues an otherwise interesting came

Bellows-type wooden folding camera; by Eastman Kodak; 1885–90; $65–90.

Bellows-type wooden folding camera; 1900–10; $40–60.

Bellows-type wooden folding camera; by G. Desse; Namur, France; 1875–85; $140–200.

Box camera, the Midge; 1910–20; $75–95.

Box camera in metal case, the Dollar Camera; by Ansco; 1920–30; $35–50.

Box camera, the Brownie No. 2, in original box; by Eastman Kodak; 1900–10; $45–65. The original box increases the value of this camera 100 percent.

Box camera; by Eastman Kodak; 1910–15; $15–25.

Box camera, the Pocket Kodak; by Eastman Kodak; ca. 1895; $60–80. This small box camera is a great favorite with collectors.

Box cameras; by
Eastman Kodak. *Left:*
Bulls Eye; 1896–1900;
$35–50. *Right:*
Brownie Box No. 2;
1900–10; $15-25.

Box camera, the Kewpie; by Conley
Camera Co.; 1900–10; $20–30.

Box cameras; by
Eastman Kodak. *Left:*
Junior Premo No. 1;
1903–06; $40–55. *Righ*
Brownie No. 0; 1898–
1905; $15–25.

Box cameras; by Eastman Kodak.
Left: Junior No. 1; 1900–06; $60–85.
Right: Brownie No. 2; 1925–35; $20–30.

Box camera; by Eastman Kodak; 1885–90; $30–45.

▲
Box camera, the Bullet Speed; by Eastman Kodak; 1897–1900; $50–70.

Box camera; unmarked but patented; 1903; $70–95. A very well built camera.

Box camera, the B2 Shur Shot, with original box; by Agfa; 1930–40; $25–40.

Box camera, the Shur Shot Special; by Agfa; 1935–45; $18–32.

Box camera, the Brownie Model C; by Eastman Kodak; with carrying case; 1940–50; $25–35. ▼

Box cameras made of ▲ plastic and metal; 1950–60. *Left:* Brownie Fiesta; by Eastman Kodak; $5–10. *Right:* Imperial; $8–14.

Left: Art Deco Bantam; by Eastman Kodak; 1935–40; $35–45. *Right:* Special World's Fair Edition; by Eastman Kodak; 1964–65; $15–22. ▼

▲ Box camera, the Roy Rogers Snap Shot; by Herbert George Co.; 1945–55; $20–30.

Reflex camera, the Ciro Flex; Delaware, Ohio; 1935–45; $60–75.

Reflex camera, the Anscoflex, with original box; by Ansco; 1950–60; $45–60.

Reflex camera, Coronet; England; 1940–50; $50–75.

Folding camera with wood and leather bellows, the Wizard; by Manhattan Optical Co.; 1890–1900; $60–80. Missing lens. ▼

Folding camera; 1890–1900; $35–50. Missing lens.

Folding camera, the ▲ Premo; by Eastman Kodak; 1903–08; $35–55.

Folding camera; the Autographic Brownie; by Eastman Kodak; 1920–30; $25–35.

Folding cameras; by Eastman Kodak.
Left: Autographic; 1902–05; $22–34.
Right: Autographic; 1909–12; $15–24.

Folding camera, the Brownie Hawk
Eye Autographic; by Eastman Kodak;
1925–35; $25–35.

Folding camera, the Cronos; by
Ernemann; 1925–35; $65–90.

Folding camera, the
Anastigmat Spector; by
Lumiere; France; 1910–
20; $80–120.

Folding camera, the
Anastigmat Special;
Eastman Kodak; 1930–
35; $45–65.

Folding camera, the Vigilant Junior;
by Eastman Kodak; 1925–35; $30–45.
With Kodet lens.

Folding camera, the Autographic
Model C; by Eastman Kodak; 1920–
30; $22–30.

Folding camera, the Anastigmat,
with Art Deco black and silver
metal case; by Eastman Kodak;
1930–40; $50–75.

Folding camera, the Clipper, with
original box and advertising material;
by Ansco; 1950–55; $30–45.

35mm camera; by Leica; 1920–30; $200–325.

35mm camera, the Minolta 35; by Minolta; 1950–60; $125–175. A Japanese version of the Leica.

35mm camera; U.S.S.R.; 1945–55; $75–105. A Russian version of the Leica.

35mm camera, the Anastigmat; by Argus; 1930–40; $25–35.

35mm camera, the Bantam Special; by Eastman Kodak; 1936–40; $75–125. The sleek Art Deco lines of this aluminum-bodied camera make it a great favorite with collectors.

Left: 35mm camera, the Speedex, in plastic case; by Agfa; 1950–55; $35–55. *Right:* Fed Flash; 1945–55; $10–18.

Folding camera; by Polaroid Co,; 1950–55; $185–230.

16mm movie camera, the Cine Kodak; by Eastman Kodak; 1925–35; $80–105.

9.5mm movie camera; by Pathe; 1925–35; $40–55. The 9.5mm movie camera never attained much popularity, and few models are available.

Left: 16mm movie camera; by Briskin; 1930–40; $65–80. *Right:* 16mm movie camera; by Keystone; 1945–55; $45–65.

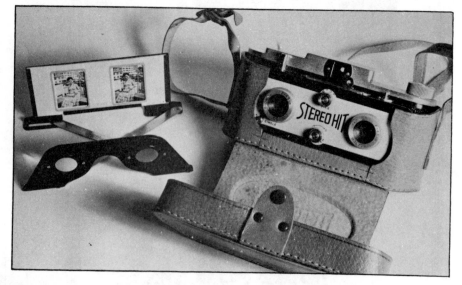

35mm stereoscopic camera, the Stereohit; Japan; 1950–60; $60–80. Today they're only a novelty, but stereohit slides were once an important addition to almost every home.

Left: Miniature camera, the Pixie; by Whitaker Manufacturing Co.; 1930–40; $15–25. *Right:* Miniature camera, the Midget, in walnut-size plastic case; by Coronet; 1936–40; $20–30.

Miniature camera, the Toyoca 16; Japan; 1950–60; $15–25.

Miniature camera, the Mycro; 1948–55; $12–18.

Miniature camera, the Diplomat; Japan; 1950–60; $10–20.

Miniature camera, the Emson; Japan; 1945–55; $8–16.

Jigsaw puzzle in the shape of a camera packed in a camera-shaped box; 1935–45; $15–24.

All-metal box camera, the Self Worker; by France & Etranger; France; 1905–15; $125–165. Made for the English and American markets.

Plastic child's toy camera; 1950–60; $1–2.

Clocks and Watches

Unless he or she chooses to collect nonfunctioning timepieces, the clock and watch enthusiast is faced with a problem seldom encountered in other fields of collectibles: making his or her acquisitions work. Nonworking clocks and watches are often quite inexpensive, but having them repaired frequently poses an economic impossibility. Another challenge to the collector is size, particularly if his or her interest is in earlier clocks. Until late in the nineteenth century, most clocks were large, and only a small number of pre-1880 wall and shelf clocks can be accommodated in the average modern home.

The problem of size can be eliminated to a great extent by choosing to collect clocks of the period from 1880 to 1950. By the end of the nineteenth century clockmaking, which as early as 1807 had become a factory business in the United States, was so refined that functional clockworks could be housed within very small cases. As a result, there is an abundance of moderate-size, interesting wall and shelf clocks from the period.

Some of these timepieces can be found in wooden cases, such as the walnut-veneered ogee-frame rectangular clocks that were produced from the 1840s until the mid-1850s. There are also the round or square oak wall clocks that were common in schools and factories from 1910 until the Second World War. Many other materials were used in clock cases. Metal—whether tin, pot metal, cast iron, brass, or stainless steel—is common, as are glass, marble, and the various plastics intended to imitate either marble or tortoiseshell.

Clock shapes are also diverse. The plain round case can be found on clocks dating from 1880 to 1950, but many other styles have had their day of glory. Among these are the large, figurine-mounted mantel clocks made by Ansonia, which offered the buyer an opportunity to purchase both a clock and a figure of anyone from Attila the Hun to Rubens.

Animated clocks were popular during both the late 1800s and the 1930s. In these rare and highly collectible timepieces the movement of the clockwork causes figures to move. As an example, soon after the end of Prohibition, American clockmakers produced a clock incorporating a figure that drank beer as the time passed.

Late-nineteenth-century forms include jigsaw-cut frames in the Eastlake style as well as rectilinear examples in the Mission style popular around 1900. As these examples indicate, clockcases frequently mirror changes in furniture design, and clock styles range from the flowing, natural forms of the Art Nouveau era to the severely geometric plastic and chrome forms of Art Deco. The latter period, which encompasses the introduction of sophisticated electric clocks, is a particularly attractive one for collectors. Both American and European timepieces are available in large numbers, and many styles can be found at moderate prices. Moreover, a higher percentage of the available clocks are functional than is the case with earlier examples.

Although many interesting clocks by minor manufacturers can be found—and should certainly not be passed up if the price is right—most collectors seek out the products of the major American factories such as Ansonia, Seth Thomas, New Haven, and Waterbury.

The oldest of these companies, the Seth Thomas Clock Company, was founded in 1813 by the pioneer clockmaker Seth Thomas. Incorporated in 1853, the company is still in business as a branch of Talley Industries. For some years, however, it has employed foreign-made parts in its clocks. Seth Thomas timepieces are well made and the most popular of collectible American clocks.

Another well-known manufacturer was the Ansonia Clock Company, which was established in Derby, Connecticut, in 1850 and moved to Brooklyn, New York, in 1879. From 1879 until 1929, Ansonia produced a vast quantity of novelty and figural clocks as well as many marble mantle clocks.

Two other giants of the industry are the New Haven Clock Company (manufacturer of the largest variety of late-nineteenth-century clocks), which was active from 1853 until 1960, and the Waterbury Clock Company (active from 1857 to 1944), which made fine calendar clocks as well as various alarm, schoolhouse, and ship's timepieces.

Because of the smaller size involved, watches present greater production problems than do clocks. For many years the United States imported watches, and before the creation of the Boston Watch Company (1853 to 1856), there were no factory-made American watches. Moreover, even after more successful competitors, such as the still existent Waltham Watch Company, entered the field, their products were for many years too expensive for most potential users. Jeweled and cased in silver and gold, throughout most of the Victorian period watches remained the prized possessions of a few. As a result, collectible watches from the pre-1880 period are generally expensive.

In 1880, the Waterbury Clock Company produced a nonjeweled watch that could be sold for only $3.75, and by 1893 Robert H. Ingersoll was selling pocket watches (at first made for him by Waterbury) for only one dollar each. Ingersoll's slogan, "The watch that made the dollar famous," heralded a new day in watch manufacture. His company and others, such as Ingraham and the company that is now Westclox, turned out thousands of inexpensive watches, all of which are now collector's items.

There was no letup, of course, in the manufacture of better, more expensive watches, and jeweled timepieces by such makers as Seth Thomas, Waltham, Elgin, and Hamilton can be found. The variety of these timepieces, particularly those made after 1900, is very great. They offer a fertile field for the collector.

The novice collector may be surprised at his inability to locate early wristwatches. The answer is simple: there were none. Other than a few late-nineteenth-century pendant watches intended for use by women, pocket watches were the sole personal timepiece until after the First World War. Collectible wristwatches, accordingly, date to the 1920s and 1930s.

Also—and this is due primarily to the limitations imposed by their small size—watches show little of the variety of design evidenced in clocks. Though they may be cased in precious metals or encrusted with gems, most watches look pretty much the same from the 1880s right through the 1940s. There are, of course, subtle changes, and one can perceive influences such as Art Nouveau and Art Deco. The important differences among such timepieces are usually found in the backplate engraving. Many watches were given as gifts and were suitably engraved. Others were engraved in commemoration of historic events, from the St. Louis World's Fair of 1904 to the New York World's Fair of 1939. Commemorative watchcases alone could form a sizable and interesting collection.

Unusually large thirty-day windup, oak cased wall clock; by Seth Thomas; 1910–20; $275–350.

Victorian shelf clock in walnut case, Model No. 1; by New Haven Clock Co.; 1880–90; $275–330. Victorian clocks are usually large and ornate.

Neoclassical shelf clock in walnut case; 1890–1900; $185–260. Clocks in the shape of temples, towers and even log cabins were very popular at the turn of the century.

Shelf clock in silver gilt pot-metal case; 1905–1? $80–125.

Alarm clock in gold-washed pot-metal case; 1890–1910; $35–60. Pot metal was often employed in inexpensive late-Victorian clocks.

Art Nouveau shelf clock in silvered pot-metal case; 1900–10; $75–105. An attractive clock decorated with glass bead inserts.

Eight-day clock in bronze and enamel case; by Schild & Co.; 1920–30; $175–225. A sophisticated clock in the early Art Deco style.

Dresser clock in imitation tortoiseshell case; 1930–40; $45–65. Clocks such as this were often part of a dresser set.

Clock and table lamp combination in bronzed pot metal; 1935–45; $75–110. Clock and lamp combinations are rare and generally of recent vintage.

Art Nouveau mantel clock in bronzed pot-metal and marbleized pottery case; by Seth Thomas; 1920–30; $100–150.

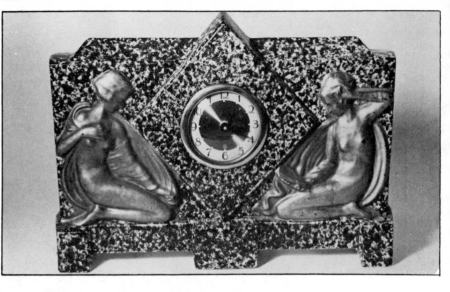

Cymric pattern mantel clock in sterling silver case; by Liberty Manufacturing Co.; 1900–10; $1,600–2,200. In the Arts and Crafts style, cymric clocks are rare and and expensive.

Mantel clock in brass and pink marble case; by Charpentier; 1920–30; $235–325.

Shelf clock in stamped brass and ▲ marble case; 1930–40; $70–110.

Coach clock in brass and glass case with original carrying case; 1885–1900; $250–335.

Art Deco electric clock in chrome and blue glass case; by Charlton; 1930–40; $55–75.

Mantel clock in glass and chrome case; by Waltham Clock Co.; 1935–45; $75–115. An extremely stylish clock in the late Art Deco style.

Shelf clock in glass and metal case; by Telechron; 1925–35; $300–400. Designed by Franckle.

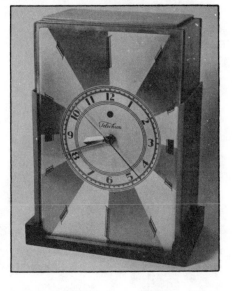

Shelf clock in metal and plastic bamboo-motif case; 1930–40; $65–85.

Eight-day clock in gold metal and glass case; 1935–45; $46–65.

Desk clock in blue plastic case with white hands; 1935–45; $40–60.

Calendar clock in metal
and Bakelite case; by
Hammond; 1935–50;
$55–65.

Alarm clock in pewter
case, the Mammoth; by
Parker Clock Co.; 1900–
10; $45–55.

Left: Miniature alarm
clock; by Ansonia Clock
Co.; 1878–85; $60–70.
Right: Alarm clock, the
Dot Alarm; by Waterbury
Clock Co.; 1925–30; $35–
45.

Sylvia pattern dresser
clock; by Seth Thomas;
1910–15; $30–35. Made
of Bakelite and brass, thi
clock is a forerunner of
the modern bedside
clock.

Alarm clock, the Royal;
by Waterbury Clock Co.;
1930–40; $40–50. Like
most alarm clocks, this
one has a body of sheet
tin.

Alarm clock in red and yellow plastic case; by New Haven Clock Co.; 1925–35; $25–30.

Art Deco cigarette lighter and clock combination in chrome and plastic; by Ronson; 1920–30; $40–50.

Wall clock in oak case; 1900–10; $90–100. Until replaced by electric clocks in the 1930s, spring-driven wall clocks were customary in every office and public building.

Hanging wall clock in oak and brass case; by Seth Thomas; 1915–25; $80–100.

Wall clock in oak case; 1920–30; $115–145.

Ship's clock in brass case; by
Waterbury Clock Co.; 1900–20;
$275–350.

Pocket watch in silver case; by Waltham Watch Co.;
1920–30; $100–135.

Pocket watches in gold-filled cases; 1925–35. *Left:* By
Waltham Watch Co.; $135–155. *Center:* By Oscar
Fresard; Lucerne, Switzerland; $250–350. *Right:* By
Hamilton; $250–325.

Left: Pocket watch in gold-filled case; by Elgin; 1930–40; $80–110. *Right:* Miniature pocket watch in gold-filled case; 1900–10; $185–240.

Pocket watch in gold and silver case; by Waltham Watch Co.; 1930–40; $150–210.

Woman's watch in the form of a pendant; Switzerland; 1920–30; $70–115. Before the development of the wristwatch, women wore watches on chains or pinned to their clothing.

Pocket watches in gold-filled cases; 1920–35. *Left:* By Elgin; $350–425. *Right:* Switzerland; $360–440.

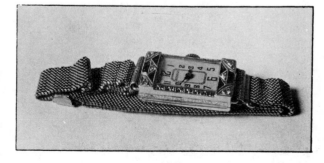

Women's wristwatch in gold-filled case; by Benrus; 1930–40; $300–400.

Woman's watch in silver case in the form of a ring; 1910–20; $110–125.

219

Indian Crafts

Interest in Indian crafts dates back to the late nineteenth century, but it has only been within the past decade or so that demand has reached the present fever pitch. Today, any well-made example, be it rug, basket, or bowl, commands a good price even if it was made only a few years ago. In part, this heightened interest is traceable to increased curiosity about all things Indian; in part, it reflects the current national craze for craft objects in general.

There are five major areas of Indian collectibles—pottery, basketry, rugs, beadwork, and wood carving—and all five are marked by certain characteristics that make them special in today's world: the items are all one of a kind, handmade, and constructed of natural materials. In our plastic, production-line society, these elements alone are enough to set Indian crafts apart.

Some American pottery can be dated back over two thousand years, but the bulk of collectible pieces were made between 1900 and 1970. Moreover, although archaeological excavations have shown that fine pottery was once made throughout the country, most examples now come from the pueblos of the Southwest.

The Indians of New Mexico and Arizona traditionally have formed their ware from coiled clay and baked it in open fires fed with goat dung. Decoration consists of abstract, geometric designs painted on the surface before firing or of similar patterns cut or scratched into a solid colored background.

Perhaps the best known of this pottery is the black-on-black ware made at the San Ildefonso pueblo near Santa Fe, New Mexico, by the Martinez family. In the early 1930s, Julian Martinez rediscovered the ancient method of smothering the baking fire to produce a rich matte black surface. From then until his death in 1943, Julian and Maria Martinez worked together (unusual in itself because most Indian potters are female), making their distinctive and usually signed pieces.

Today, with other members of the family, Maria carries on.

Black glaze pottery is not typical of the Southwest. Most ware from that area is glazed in several colors—red, yellow, black, and white are the most common—and is burned in an oxygen-rich fire to produce light colors. Typical of the area are the fine examples made at the pueblos of Santa Clara, Santo Domingo, and Acoma in New Mexico and among the Hopi Indians of Arizona.

Light and durable, basketry items are important to any primitive society, and Indians throughout North America have always made them in large quantities. In the extreme Northeast, the Passamaquoddy and Micmac tribes of northern New England still manufacture a great variety of splint and sweet-grass baskets, as do the Iroquois of central New York. Among the tribes of the Southeast, pine needles and sugarcane have served as materials. In most cases, basketry is produced both for personal use and as something to be sold to tourists.

Without doubt, the finest Indian baskets and the ones most sought by collectors are those of the Southwest. The tightly coiled baskets, bowls, trays, and jars of the California Pomo, Yurok, and Washo tribes are made of a variety of materials, including cedar bark, grass, leaves, and even roots all woven together with a remarkable facility. The fine construction and powerful, abstract decoration of these containers have a strong appeal to collectors—so strong, in fact, that certain more desirable examples have sold for over a thousand dollars apiece. Other well-known baskets of the Southwest are produced by the Apache, Navajo, Paiute, and Hopi.

Because of the nature of the materials from which they are constructed, baskets have a short life, and the great majority of them on the market today date to the 1920s or even later. What the collector should focus on here is not age but quality of design and construction.

The strong patterns and vivid colors of Western Indian blankets and rugs have had a great attraction for collectors for a long time. Although the Zuni and Hopi have made some appealing examples, most enthusiasts seek out Navajo textiles. The Navajo weavers work on an upright loom of their own invention and employ natural dyes and wool from their own sheep. Before the turn of the century they made blankets both for their own use and as trade goods. These were usually rectangular and vertically striped, although certain more elaborate pieces, called chief's blankets, were squarish in shape.

As the nineteenth century waned, however, an influx of factory-made blankets made blanket weaving unnecessary. Fortunately, it was at this time that whites began to buy the textiles as wall hangings. From this it was a natural step to producing thicker pieces as floor coverings. Since 1900 the Navajo have made a wide variety of rugs, some pictorial, some geometric, but all highly collectible. Indian rugs and blankets are today treated as art forms to be hung alongside the finest modern paintings.

Though perhaps less well known than the other Indian crafts, beadwork is important not only for its artistic merit but also because it is unique to the American Indian. When the first whites arrived in this country they found Indians decorating clothing and making small containers from porcupine quills. Dyed and flattened, these quills were sewn to background material in a variety of different patterns. When trade beads became available, the native craftsmen quickly began to employ these in their complex, essentially geometric designs.

Eastern Indian beadwork is characterized by rounded, floral designs while that of the Western tribes (such as the Shoshone, Comanche, and Sioux) leans more to geometric forms. Earlier examples, made for tribal use, include beaded pipe and gun bags, moccasins, and gauntlets. Later pieces, made during the period from 1910 to 1950, were often intended for sale to tourists and range from pincushions to watch fobs and souvenir pieces such as those still made by the Indians residing in the vicinity of Niagara Falls.

Indian crafts also include wood carving. The tribes of the Northwestern coast of North America, particularly the Haida and the Kwakiutl, are among the finest wood sculptors of all time. Masks, totems, chests, and carved eating utensils from this area have long been sought by museums and private collectors. Today, most pre-1940 examples are unavailable, but later pieces still come on the market. The only comparable work found in the Northeast are the false faces or medicine-man masks made by the Iroquois of New York. These too are well carved and would be a valuable addition to any collection.

Another form of wood carving is the kachinas of the Southwestern pueblos. Shaped from cottonwood and ranging in size from a few inches to several feet, kachinas are either masks or fully developed figures. In either case they represent figures from the Indian spirit world. Since there are over five hundred such deities, there are a great many pieces to be found, some dating back as far as 1880. However, the collector should be on guard against wood and even plastic or clay reproductions manufactured in Asia and sold at tourist shops throughout the West.

Other collectible Indian craft objects include hand-hammered silver, often mounted with turquoise or coral; elaborately decorated leather clothing; and wooden objects, such as rattles, drums, and weapons. All represent important areas of the collectibles field.

Pottery bowl in red, black, and white; Acoma Pueblo; ca. 1920; $120–160. A relatively common but attractive example.

Pottery bowl in black and white lightning pattern; Miembres culture; Southwestern United States; 13th century; $225–265. Bowls like this were the forerunners of modern American Indian pottery.

Alphabet bowl in polished black clay; Cherokee; 1910–15; $230–310. Signed Bigmeat.

Left: Pottery bowl in red and gray; Santa Clara Pueblo; 1930–40; $55–85. *Right:* Pottery bowl in tan and black; Hopi; 1925–35; $75–125.

Sculptured clay bowl polished black; Santa Clara Pueblo; 1920–30; $85–145.

Pottery bowl with elaborate geometric
pattern in black and orange on white;
Zuni; 1935–45; $145–215.

Pottery figure of a rain god in red,
black, and white; Tesuque Pueblo;
1940–45; $30–50.

Woven-grass basket stained in red; Tulare; 1880–90;
$650–850. A very early and finely made example of
California basketry.

Woven basket, black on tan; Pima;
1870–80; $475–540.

Woven-grass hats; Hupa; 1880–90;
$120–155 each.

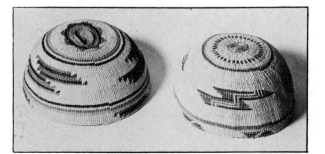

Large basketry olla, or jar; Apache; 1900–05; $1,600–2,100. Examples of this size and artistic merit are hard to obtain today.

Woven-grass bowl, brown on tan; Papago; 1940–50; $100–165.

Woven basketry bowls, brown and tan; Papago; 1935–45. *Left:* $90–130. *Right:* $125–170. Pictorial designs enhance the value of the piece at right.

Wide, flat basket decorated with abstract human figure; Pima; 1890–1900; $275–375.

Covered basketry water jar; Papago; ; 1910–20; $240–320. This piece is so tightly woven it will hold water.

Sweet-grass and splint baskets; Penobscot; 1940–55. *Left:* $20–30. *Center:* $22-33. *Right:* $30–40. The Maine Indians have long specialized in finely woven miniature baskets, many of which are less than three inches in diameter.

Interior of splint sewing basket; Micmac; 1930–35; $75–115.

Covered sweet-grass basket in unusual octagonal design; Penobscot; 1935–45; $40–55. Bands of stained grass in pink and green highlight this basket.

Woven-grass basket; Micmac; 1945–55; $55–70.

False face society mask of wood, carved and painted white with applied horsehair; Iroquois; ca. 1900; $1,750–2,750. These rare masks were carved for members of the tribe's medicine-man group.

False face society mask of wood, painted black and red with applied black horsehair; Iroquois; 1900–1($1,800–,2,700.

Wooden mask, carved and painted red, black, green, and white; Kwakiutl; 1890–1900; $6,000–8,500. The Indians of the Northwest Coast are among the world's finest sculptors.

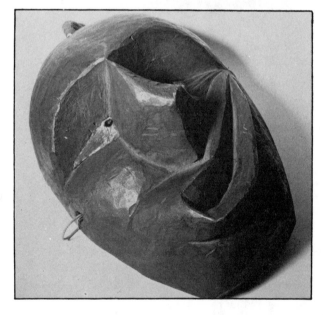

False face society mask of wood, carved and painted red; Oneida; 1890–1900; $2,600–3,000.

Canvas and wood tableta, or ceremonial headdress, in red, yellow, blue, and white; Southwest; 1920–25; $700–850.

Ceremonial bowl, carved wood painted red and black; Northwest Coast; 1890–1900; $1,600–2,000.

Totem figure, or "house key," pine carved and painted black; Shimshim; 1890–1900; $900–1,100.

...rved wooden ...re; Haida; ...0–90; $1,800– ...50. Small ...res such as ...se were given ...gifts at ceremo-...l feasts, or ...laches.

Ceremonial bowl, unpainted pine inlaid with cowrie shell; 1870–80; $7,500–10,000. Pieces of this quality are rare and expensive.

Canoe thwart carved in the form of a human face with traces of red and blue paint; Northwest Coast; 19th century; $2,300–2,800.

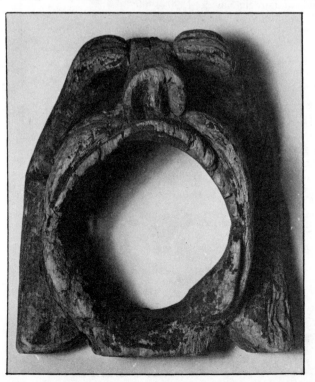

Totem pole with red, white, blue, and black paint; Tlingit; 1890–1900; $3,200–3,600.

Fin from ceremonial carving of killer whale, pine with traces of red and green paint; Northwest Coast 19th century; $1,900–2,200.

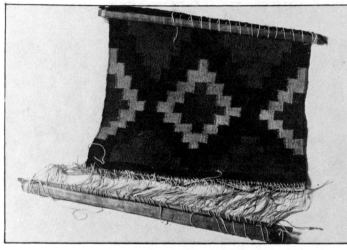

Miniature mat or weaving in Germantown pattern, red, orange, black, and green; Navajo; 1890–1900; $145–185. The Navajo made miniatures such as this for sale to tourists.

Rug in "eye dazzler" Germantown pattern, red, black, white, and yellow; Navajo; 1895–1900; $1,400–1,900. From the so-called classical period.

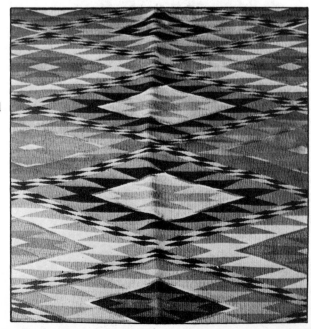

Wool rug dyed red, tan, black, and white; Navajo; 1920–25; $500–650. The Navajos have produced the finest Indian textiles.

Rug in zigzag pattern, gray, yellow, white, and black; Navajo; 1905–15; $650–900.

TicNosPas rug dyed red, black, white, orange, blue, and gray; Navajo; 1910–20; $750–1,100.

Yei rug in gray, white, and black; Navajo; 1930–35; $550–850.

Germantown pattern double saddle blanket, red, yellow, blue, and green. Navajo; 1880–90; $650–700.

Beaded panels for a small carrying bag; Eastern Woodlands; 19th century; $275–350 the pair. The skillful blending of red, pink, blue, and white beads in this work is typical of high-quality Indian beadwork.

Beaded bag in red, white, and green beads on green leather; Kiowa; 1890–1900; $110–145.

Beaded moccasin in red, white, blue, and yellow; Sioux; 1880–90; $125–175.

Beaded martingale for horse; Nez Perce; 1880–90; $900–1,200. This remarkably elaborate example combines tiny brass bells, mother-of-pearl, and seashells, with red, white, blue, pink, and black beads.

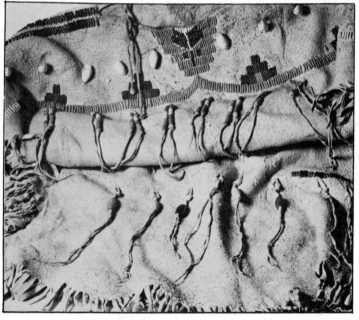

Beaded shirt decorated with cowrie shells and red, orange, blue, yellow, and pink beads; Plateau; 1920–25; $200–300.

Beaded pipe bag; Cheyenne; 1880–85; $450–650. This bag is decorated with dyed porcupine quills and red, yellow, and blue beads.

Pincushion embellished with red, white, and blue beads; Iroquois; dated 1919; $35–45. For many years the Indians of western New York have made beadwork pieces such as this for sale to tourists.

Beadwork wall pocket in tan, white, and green; Iroquois; 1920–35; $40–55.

Beadwork wall pocket, white beads on tan cloth; Iroquois; 1935–45; $20–30.

Woven leather bait bag decorated with red and blue beads and bone toggle; American Eskimo; 1880–90; $250–350.

Silver concha belt set with turquoise; Navajo; 1940–45; $750–900.

231

Turquoise and silver bracelet; Navajo; 1890–1900; $1,000–1,450. Old silver like this is often called pawn, because it was frequently pawned by the Indians during the periods between crops.

Pawn silver bracelets; Navajo. *Left:* Set with turquoise; 1900–10; $350–475. *Right:* Set with turquoise and coral; 1910–20; $265–330.

Miniature canoe of birch bark and quill work; Micmac; 1880–1900; $120–160.

Silver bracelet set with turquoise; Navajo; 1920–25; $275–375.

Doll with leather dress decorated in pink, green, yellow, and blue beads; Cree; 1880–90; $750–1,000. Pre-1900 Indian dolls are extremely rare.

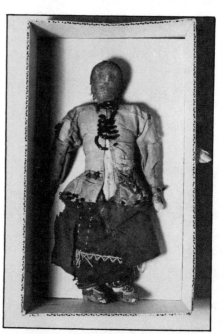

Pipes made of catlinite, a form of red soapstone;
Plains; 1890–1910. *Left:* $40–60. *Right:* $90–125.

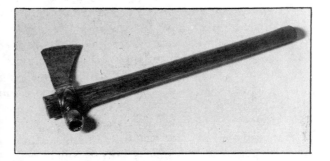

Wrought-iron trade axe and pipe combination; 18th
century; $1,200–1,800.

Knife and case; Kwakiutl; 1870–80; $1,800–2,200. The
blade has been cut down from a Russian saber, and the
head is carved in the form of a totem bear.

Fetish made from an
animal vertebrae painted
red, blue, and green;
Southwest; 1920–25;
$120–155. Intended to be
worn around the neck.

Sports Memorabilia

Sports collectibles, a field of great interest and variety, comprise a rapidly growing sector of interest—particularly for the male collector.

Perhaps the oldest and certainly the most popular area today is hunting memorabilia. Sporting firearms, rifles and shotguns, have been collected for a long time, and few antiquarians are unaware of such fine items as Kentucky rifles and carved powder horns. But these things are both scarce and expensive, so the contemporary collector must look elsewhere. Many fine examples of sporting arms were made between 1880 and 1940 by such prestigious manufacturers as Stevens and Remington. Interesting items such as octagonal-barreled .22 caliber rifles and double-barreled shotguns may be purchased quite reasonably. Of course, as with military arms, one should bear in mind that functioning weapons are subject to state licensing laws.

Associated gunning paraphernalia, such as powder horns, bullet molds, loading tools, and game bags, are also collectible, as are trophies, which range from the usual set of deer antlers to gigantic, stuffed and mounted moose heads. As to the latter, however, keep in mind that under Federal law it is unlawful to own certain bird trophies (such as hawks and eagles) even though they were mounted long ago.

Decoys are very popular with sports enthusiasts today. These full-size replicas of ducks, shorebirds, crows, and even owls, were usually carved from wood, though examples in tin, papier-mâché, and even plastic can be found. Originally intended to deceive waterfowl, they are now perceived as folk art or, in the words of an early collector, Joel Barber, as "utilitarian, floating sculpture."

Duck decoys are the most common type, with some thirty-four different species having been duplicated. The most commonly seen types are the black duck, canvasback, redhead, and Canada goose. Less available are tiny shorebirds, such as curlews and plovers. Unlike duck decoys, which were designed to float on the water, these shorebird decoys were mounted on a stick that could be stuck in the ground. Since shorebird hunting was largely outlawed over fifty years ago, these decoys are hard to come by, and the enthusiast should be wary of recent reproductions and outright fakes.

Pigeon, owl, and crow decoys are less often seen but are regarded as quite desirable by some collectors. Many of these decoys were produced in factories (as were some duck and shorebird decoys), and they are usually inexpensive.

Until recently, fishing collectibles were for the most part ignored by collectors. Now, however, the craftsmanship of the old-time reel and rod makers has come to be appreciated by a growing number of enthusiasts. Fly rods, those long, slim bamboo wands, which can delicately drop a tiny fly on the water dozens of feet from the caster, were made one by one by men such as Hiram Lewis Leonard and Edward Payne. These makers have come to be recognized as true artists in their field. Their products were not cheap when new, and at present may sell for hundreds of dollars apiece. For the more modest collector there are the production-line rods turned out in the 1920s and 1930s by such well-known fishing-tackle factories as James Heddon & Sons and the South Bend Bait Company.

The reels that held the fishing line are also of interest, particularly the pre-1900 handcrafted models by makers such as Julius Vom Hofe and Yawman & Erbe. Though collectors are seeking nearly all pre-1940 reels, they particularly desire the giant salmon reels and the tiny (less than two inches in diameter) "midge" trout reels.

Nets, fly boxes, and even trout flies are also considered fair game for collectors. As in the area of hunting memorabilia, paintings or sculpture of fish or fishing scenes are considered to be of great interest. The field of fishing memorabilia is growing fast, but there is still a good chance for the new collector to get in on the ground floor.

For many people, horse racing is the number-one American sport, and when one adds to the millions who follow the "sport of kings" the many thousands who ride for pleasure, it becomes evident that a vast number of people have some interest in horse-related memorabilia. For many this involves no more than collecting some of the many prints or paintings that depict horses or horse-racing scenes. For others, however, such memorabilia is supplemented by actual riding gear, such as crops, riding caps, jockey silks, bits, bridles, spurs, and—naturally—the ubiquitous horseshoe. Though such items as Spanish silver spurs and early Western saddles can be fabulously expensive, most racing and riding collectibles can be purchased rather inexpensively. This is particularly true of associated items such as bookends, ashtrays, and the like, depicting or made in the form of horses or horse heads. These pieces alone can provide the nucleus of a good collection.

A much newer area is that of hobby or amateur sailing. For many years collectors have been interested in mementoes of the great days of sailing ships—scrimshaw, whaling gear, clipper ship models and paintings, and naval weapons—but only recently have collectors become aware of the interesting relics associated with small-boat sailing.

The most obviously appealing collectibles here are models of famous racers such as the *America*, first winner of the cup that bears its name. These can be either fully rigged or of the flat-backed type known as "half models." Equally popular are paintings or lithographs of racing scenes.

A fortunate few can afford to collect the boats themselves, but for most collectors the equipment used aboard the boats will have to do. This includes such items as compasses, wheels, porthole covers, sextants, and even the binoculars used by the men or women on watch. Since many of these items are made wholly or in part of brass, they make attractive additions to the den or living room.

In a nation as sports minded as this one, the vast field of sporting memorabilia must inevitably continue to expand. Everything from hockey sticks to mountain-climbing gear will eventually become collectible, and the wise collector or dealer will purchase these things now while many can still be found at relatively low prices—a situation that can't last forever.

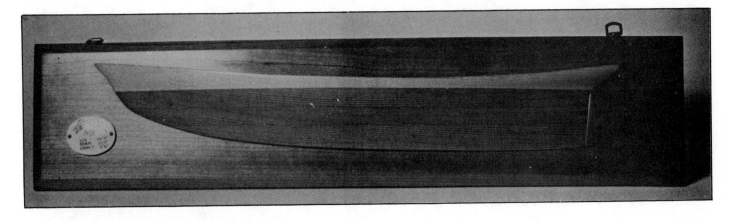

Wooden half model of the racing vessel *America*, winner of the first America's Cup; 1960–65; $145–175.

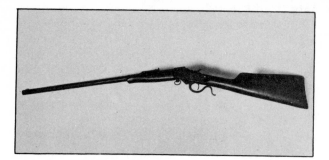

Single-shot .22 caliber sporting rifle; by Winchester; 1890–1910; $75–110. The .22 was the traditional "boys rifle" during the Victorian era just as it is today.

Single-barreled 12 gauge shotgun; by Union Arms Co.; Toledo, Ohio; 1905–15; $70–95.

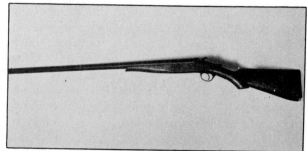

Double-barreled 16 gauge shotgun; by Gordon Gun Co.; 1920–30; $90–140.

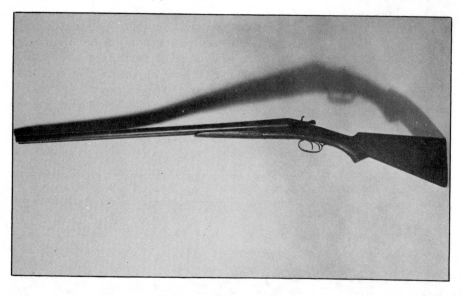

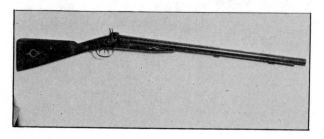

Buckshot mold, iron and wood; 1880–1900; $45–75.

Double-barreled fowling piece or shotgun with silver and brass inlay; 1860–85; $275–350.

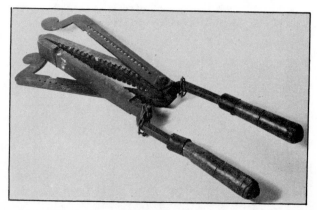

Bronze sporting sculpture, "Hunter with Stag"; by H. Malle; 1875–90; $750–900.

Bronze sporting sculpture, "Hunter with Dog"; by H. Malle; 1875–90; $800–1,000.

Mallard drake decoy in black, blue, brown, and white; 1920–30; $125–150.

Duck decoys in black and white. *Left:* Bufflehead drake; 1925–30; $55–70. *Right:* Old-squaw; 1930–40; $85–115.

Red-breasted merganser decoy; 1900–10; $215-285. Well-carved decoys in old paint, such as this one, are highly prized by collectors.

White-tail scooter decoy in black and white; 1880–1900; $100–160.

Left: Broadbill decoy; 1900–10; $90–125. *Right:* Canvasback decoy; 1925–35; $60–80.

Black duck decoy in brown, gray, and black; 1910–20; $90–135.

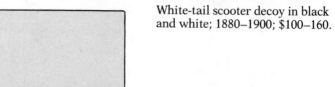

Crow decoy in black; 1950–55; $75–105. Though not very old, this is a well-shaped example.

Unidentified plastic duck decoy in brown, green, and white; 1950–55; $10–20.

238

Pigeon decoy of papier-mache; 1925–30; $20–35.
Plastic and composition decoys are generally not
popular with collectors.

Fly reels in chrome and steel; by Julius
Vom Hofe; 1889–95. *Left:* Midge;
$250–325. *Center:* Salmon; $125–165.
Right: Standard; $230–310.

Skeleton-frame fly reels. *Left:* By
Meisselbach; 1890–95; $60–85.
Center: In solid brass; by Pflue-
ger; 1930–35; $35–55. *Right:* In
black Bakelite; by Horrocks-
Ibbotson; 1940–45; $15–25.

Left: Fly reel in red Bakelite; by
Holden; 1935–45; $25–40.
Center: Skeleton reel in brass;
1920–25; $30–40. *Right:*
Automatic reel in brass; by
Yawman & Erbe; 1888–95;
$175–215.

Left: Salmon reel in chrome and steel;
by Julius Vom Hofe; 1902–12; $160–
210. *Right:* Salmon reel in chrome or
stainless steel; 1888–95; $220–280.

Fly rod probably made of ash; by William Mitchell; 1885–90; $500–600. Early nonbamboo fly rods are rare.

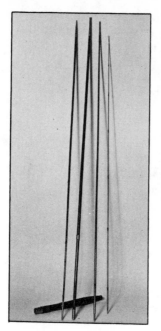

Fly rod of bamboo; by Edward Payne; 1910–20; $525–600. Payne is one of the most highly regarded of early rod makers.

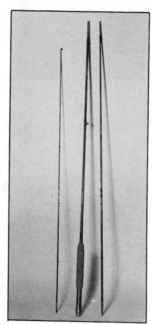

Fly rod of bamboo; by James Heddon & Sons; 1930–35; $250–325.

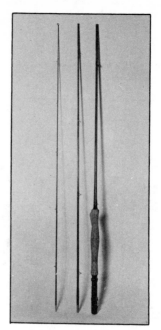

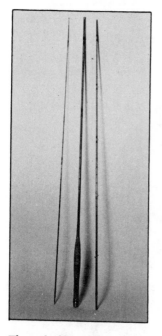

Fly rod of bamboo, Catskill model; by Hiram Lewis Leonard; 1915–20; $550–650. The Catskill line is a forerunner of the modern fly rod.

Left: Fishing net of wood; by Thomas; 1930–35; $35–45. *Right:* Collapsible fishing net in metal and wood; 1925–30; $25–35.

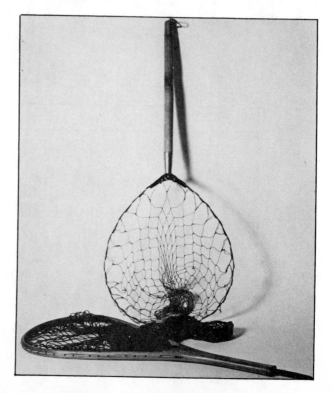

Storage box for trout flies in oak and brass; by Hardy Brothers; 1920–30; $275–350.

Genre painting of jumping brook trout; Maine; 1890–1910; $250–350. Folk paintings of fishing and hunting scenes are in great demand.

Model of a brown trout, carved and painted wood; 1910–20; $235–285.

Horse bits of cast and wrought iron; 1900–15; $7–12 each.

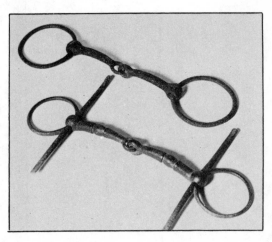

Riding cap in black wool felt, 1940–50; $30–50. Riding crop in leather, deer horn, and silver; 1900–10; $75–125.

Bookend in pot metal and wood;
1930–40; $30–40 the pair.

Bookend in painted pot metal;
1910–20; $55–80 the pair.

Miniature figure of a horse and
jockey in cast metal; by Britains;
1925–35; $25–35.

Miniature figure of a horse and jockey in painted pot
metal; 1935–40; $15–25.

Hand-tinted lithograph of a racing scene; 1880–1900;
$175–250.

Half model in wood of the racing yacht *Columbia;*
1960–65; $165–230.

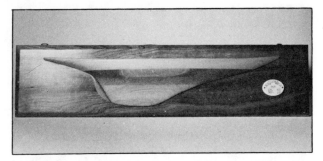

Ship's sextant in brass; 1900–10; $275–350.

Compass in brass housed in a brass
binnacle with attached oil lamp for
night use; 1880–90; $300–450.

Reprint of 19th-century Currier & Ives lithograph of
the cutter yacht *Maria;* 1930–40; $35–45. Currier &
Ives marine prints are so popular that even reprints
have substantial value.

Binoculars in
brass and steel;
1900–20. *Left:*
$60–85. *Right:*
$80–110.

Vintage Clothing

Clothing is a unique collectible because it is usually collected not simply to be admired, but also to be worn. There are, of course, collectors who maintain large costume or period clothing collections, but far more frequently the purchaser of old clothing intends to put his or her acquisition to use. Moreover, most collectors and dealers in clothing are young and live in large cities or in college communities where the wearing of period costume is acceptable and popular. Rural antiques dealers who stock early clothing usually do so in order to sell it wholesale to city merchants.

For the most part, clothing is collected by period, with some collectors favoring the Victorian look and others drawn to the slim, boyish lines of the 1920s or the flamboyant, Hollywood-inspired styles of the 1930s and 1940s. Within each era exists a multitude of interesting collectible objects.

Among women's garments, dresses and evening gowns of all periods are in great demand. Also sought after are the white undergarments of the late nineteenth and early twentieth centuries, which now are being worn, in some cases, as dresses. Hats appropriate to the costumes are also popular, especially the straw hats worn during the 1920 to 1940 era. Shoes, too, are collectible, particularly the high-button version favored during the early years of this century. Handbags and small purses may be found in numerous materials, from fur to precious metals, and these are collected or used by many people who have no interest at all in other early clothing items. Women's coats are also sought after, and such popular 1920s furs as raccoon and beaver are refurbished and worn by numerous young devotees of the "roaring twenties."

There are clothing collectibles for men as well. The trim lines and tailored look of the late Victorian period appeal to some people, though suits from this era are not easy to come by. More available are traditional blue gabardines from the 1930s and the notorious "zoot suits" popular during the late 1940s. The latter are all the rage with the disco set. Early formal wear, when it can be found, is of great interest, but few contemporary men can fit into the smaller sizes that accommodated their forefathers—a problem, incidentally, that is also often encountered by the ladies as well.

Men's hats and shoes are widely available. Among the former, bowlers and top hats are well thought of, and the disco crowd is always seeking 1930s-type snap-brim stetsons—like the gangster hats associated with the Cagney-Bogart movie era. Likewise, the brightly colored felt hats, both porkpies and the wide-brimmed feathered versions favored by zoot-suiters, are once more in style. There is some interest in the pre-1920 high-top shoes, but most buyers want either 1930s wing tips or the saddle shoes and white buckskins associated with Andy Hardy and the bucolic college movies of the period from 1940 to 1950. Neckties, too, are in vogue, particularly the garish hand-painted or silk-screened types so common shortly after the Second World War.

Though influenced on its periphery by "outsider" styles such as the jazz look of the 1930s and the zoot-suiter fad, men's clothing has remained amazingly constant in style over the past century. Such has not been the case with women's wear, and most knowledgeable collectors can date women's clothing to within a few years, going by style alone.

The earliest garments with which we are concerned—those worn at the turn of the century—reflect a life-style in which women were expected to do little other than look pretty. Beauty was conceived in terms of the classical hourglass figure, and women were expected to pad themselves or wear constricting corsets in order to achieve this norm. However, soon after 1900, designers introduced flowing garments that demanded a much slimmer figure and also could not be worn over the previously popular petticoats. Bulky undergarments were out and diet was in, a pattern that has been maintained to the present day.

By the 1920s, high waists had been replaced by styles that hugged the hips, hair was cut short beneath the close-fitting cloche hats, and dress lengths rose to heights never dreamed of during the nineteenth century. Then, in the 1930s, draping and pleating reappeared along with huge hats, a natural waist, and padded shoulders. By the late 1940s, skirts were inching up again, and padding was gone, to be replaced once more by the "natural look," which heralded the coming of dungarees and the casual clothes of the 1960s. Each stylistic variation during these periods has its devotees among clothing collectors.

Because it is used (that is, worn), clothing has problems unique in the collectibles field. To be salable, it must be in good condition or repairable. This means that most dealers and many collectors in the field are, by necessity, amateur tailors. And because it is worn, old clothing wears out. As a result, substantial numbers of early garments are destroyed every year, something that is bound to have an eventual effect on a field in which prices are already rising steadily. On the other hand, clothing is a relatively new collectible, and large quantities of desirable garments can still be found in both urban and rural areas. The collector with the patience to explore thrift shops, house sales, and church benefits will often come up with treasures that can be purchased for next to nothing. Such prizes are undoubtedly out there—it is just a matter of having the patience to seek them out.

Men's high-top shoes. *Rear:* Black leather; 1915–25; $50–70. *Front:* Brown leather; 1920–30; $50–65.

Flocked velvet dress and jacket in royal blue; 1885–1905; $275–375. The hourglass silhouette characteristic of late-19th-century fashions is clearly evident in this attractive costume.

Afternoon dress in lace-trimmed natural silk; 1910–20; $275–350.

Evening gown in gold embroidered white silk; 1920–30; $225–300.

Tea gown in accordian-pleated silk chiffon with blue velvet trim; 1920–25; $400–600. The short skirt of this lovely blue and gold garment is typical of the 1920s.

Evening dress in black silk and gauze; 1925–30; $120–160.

Tea gown in black satin and silk chiffon decorated with cut crystal and seed beads; 1920–30; $450–550. The handwork on this garment is outstanding.

Tea dress in pink silk chiffon; 1920–30; $115–145. An example of the so-called sweet-sixteen dress.

Beauclea dress in wine-colored silk; 1935–40; $125–150.

Evening gown in gauze over black-and-white pattern satin; 1950–55; $115–145.

Art Deco dress in red, black, green, and orange crepe; 1930–35; $250–350. An uncommonly sophisticated print.

Cotton housedress in red, black, green, and yellow print; 1930–40; $25–40. Sold by mail order for as little as ninety-nine cents each, these "Depression prints" are now popular with a more affluent clientele.

Evening gown in pink silk taffeta; 1930–40; $85–110.

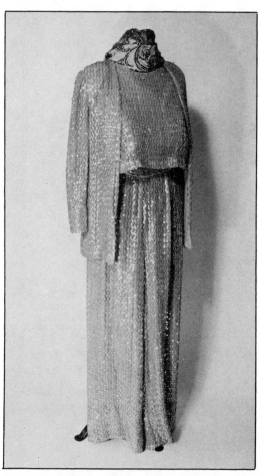

Evening gown in teal blue satin; 1950–55; $120–160.

"Mini dress" of nylon decorated with silver plastic bangles; 1960–65; $95–140.

Three-piece evening suit with pink sequins; 1950–55; $300–400. Sequined scarf; 1950–55; $15–25.

Suit in navy blue gabardine; 1935–45; $65–85.

Wool suit in black and white stripes; 1940–45; $150–185.

Victorian maternity slip in white silk; 1890–1900; $200–300. This slip is cut and pleated to provide for the growth of the baby.

Dressing gown in purple silk; 1920–25; $75–105.

Evening suit in dark blue rayon; 1930–35; $75–100.

Peignoir in pink lace and slipper satin; 1940–50; $125–150. Scarf in peach satin; 1940–50; $7–15.

Dressing gown in rust silk organza; 1950–55; $100–135.

Victorian bodice in silk decorated with jetbeads; 1880–90; $240–320.

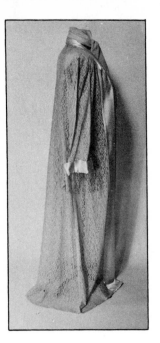

Evening sweater in natural cashmere trimmed with white fox; 1950–55; $105–135.

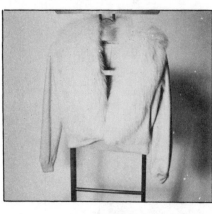

Victorian capelet in black silk with jetbead trim; 1890–1900; $125–150.

Coat in green wool trimmed with Persian lamb; 1900–10; $425–550.

Coat in maroon wool with white fox trim; 1940–45; $250–325. Blue sequined scarf; 1940–45; $10–20.

Cape in black monkey fur; 1940–45; $1,300–2,50. With the animals now protected by law, there are few monkey-fur capes available.

Left: Hat in tan felt with orange and white artificial flowers; 1930–40; $30–45. *Right:* Hat in lavender straw; 1920–30; $60–75.

Boa of silver fox; 1940–45; $275–375. Tailored jacket in tan and cream gabardine; 1940–45; $45–60.

Cloche hat in red felt; 1920–30; $35–55.

Women's straw hats; 1930–45. *Left:* Natural with artificial flowers; $25–35. *Center:* Red with blue satin ribbon; $35–50. *Right:* Natural with veil and brown ribbon; $20–30.

Turban hat in black silk chiffon; 1930–40; $28–33. A hat made famous by Marlene Dietrich.

Woman's high-laced shoe in brown leather; 1915–20; $65–85.

Left: Evening pump in black satin; 1920–25; $40–55. *Right:* Brown suede shoe; 1910–15; $80–105.

Left: Evening shoe with pink sequins; 1950–55; $55–75. *Right:* Shoe in tan and cream leather; 1920–30; $50–70. *Top:* Open-toed strap in violet material; 1930–35; $30–45.

Left: Woman's overshoe in fox, velvet, and rubber; 1940–45; $30–40. *Right:* Sling-back pump in blue suede and alligator dyed red; 1940–45; $35–55. These shoes are in the so-called Betty Grable style.

Compact case in pot metal and velvet with silk tassel; 1890–1910; $50–65.

Compact case in red plastic decorated with floral motif in cream, blue, and green; 1920–30; $35–45.

Chain purses. *Left:* Black silk with ivory handle; 1915–20; $55–68. *Center:* Black velvet with sterling silver handle; 1930–35; $60-85. *Right:* Black silk with gold sequins; 1930–40; $40–60.

Chain purses. *Left:* Jet and black sequins; 1950–55; $25–30. *Center:* Needlepoint and beadwork; 1950–55; $35–40. *Right:* Steel point tapestry with marcasite clasp; 1930–40; $65–75.

Muff and purse combination in civet; 1940–45; $25–40.

Clutch purses; 1940–50. *Left:* Black sequins; $40–55. *Center:* Red goatskin; $35–50. *Right:* Red and white coiled plastic; $15–25.

Man's overcoat of wool cashmere; 1950–55; $100–150.

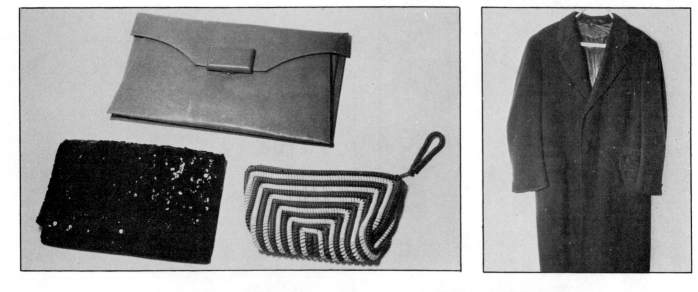

Stormcoat in tan gabardine with artificial wool collar; 1950–55; $45–55.

Raincoat in tan gabardine; 1945–55; $60–85.

Menswear; 1950–55. Jacket in white rayon; $40–55. Shirt in red cotton; $20–32. Red and black striped tie; $6–9.

Sportcoat in hand-woven yellow silk; 1950–55; $110–150.

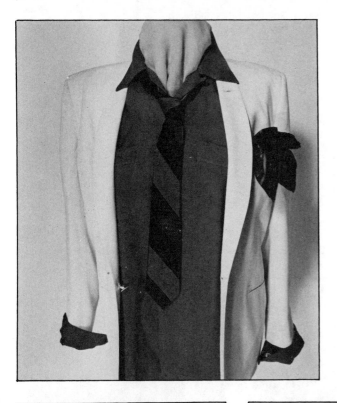

Cutaway coat in black wool; by J. Press; 1915–20; $135–165.

Jacket in black rayon; 1945–55; $50–65.

Sportcoat in cotton with red paisley pattern and brass buttons; 1955–60; $30–45.

Leisure coat in gray rayon tweed and blue gabardine; 1945–50; $40–55.

Lounge jacket in wool and nylon in gray and white; 1940–45; $25–40.

Menswear; 1930–35. Vest in yellow wool; $30–40. Shirt in cotton in blue pattern; $15–25. Blue and black bow tie; $5–10.

Pullover or Shirt-Jac in green gabardine; 1940–50; $20–32.

Top hats in felt; 1920–30; $70–110 each. The example at left is shown collapsed for storage.

Hawaiian-style shirt in red, brown, and white pattern; 1955–60; $25–35.

Left: Fedora in brown felt; 1935–40; $25–40. *Center:* Black bowler; 1920–30; $40–55. *Right:* Straw boater; 1920–30; $35–50. The fedora is the "gangster" hat of the 1930s.

Silk-screened neckties; 1940–50; $10–15 each.

Left: Black and white wing tip; 1930–35; $45–60.
Center: Brown and white shoe; $1940–50; $40–55.
Right: Brown and white saddle shoe; 1950–60; $35–5.

Left: Brown leather shoe; 1940–50; $40–60. *Right:* White buckskin; 1945–55; $30–45.

Radios, Phonographs, and Jukeboxes

Phonographs, jukeboxes, and radios pose both opportunities and problems for the collector. Radios, particularly those from the 1930s and 1940s, are relatively easy to obtain and can often be purchased for very little money. Phonographs, too, are not difficult to come by, but jukeboxes, because of both their size and cost, do not lend themselves to extensive collecting. Moreover, all these devices are frequently found in disrepair, and neither the supplies nor the expertise needed to fix them are generally available.

Although a phonographlike device was patented in 1863 by one F. B. Fenby, the first true talking machine was invented by Thomas A. Edison in 1878. The inventor applied a steel needle to a rotating tin cylinder so that the needle point cut grooves in the metal according to the intensity of the received sound. After these grooves had been cut, the original sound could be duplicated by running a needle through the grooves again.

Alexander Graham Bell, of telephone fame, refined Edison's procedure by substituting wax cylinders, which produced a higher quality sound. Wax cylinders are two to four inches long and were made in great quantities until well into the 1900s. They are collector's items in their own right, with rarer examples such as those made by the Bettini firm selling for several hundred dollars apiece.

However, when Emile Berliner, in 1887, developed the prototype for the modern, flat phonographic disc, he opened the way for the common 78, 45, and 33 rpm phonograph records of this century. Today, many of these are desirable collectibles.

Early phonographs were hand powered and depended on a spring-driven motor that was wound with a long crank handle. Before 1913, they also had large speaker horns of nickel-plated steel or tin that were attached to the outside of the talking machine. The replacement of these "morning glory" (so called for their shape) horns by interior speakers greatly changed the appearance of the phonograph.

Edison phonographs are the most sought after by collectors, and the facsimile signature of the inventor on a 1911 model Home phonograph or a 1909 Maroon Gem is highly prized. But talking machines by other manufacturers are also collectible. The 1898 Columbia Graphaphone, the Zon-O-Phone of the early 1900s, and the many Victor models are all worth looking for. Nor should one overlook the various collectible phonographic accessories. Advertisements, such as those featuring the Victor ("His master's voice") dog and the Columbia Sphinx, are in great demand, as are catalogs, brochures, and record jackets.

The jukebox is the natural culmination of the phonograph. These large, complex machines became popular in the 1930s and can accommodate numerous records, which can be played one at a time or in series. Too large and too expensive for most homes, the "jukes" were intended for use in places of public entertainment, and their styling—featuring colored neon tubing and Art Deco plastic and metal cases—was clearly designed to catch the eye of the paying public. Today, it is this very styling that catches the collector's eye.

Collectible radios are for the most part much more recent than phonographs. Although the groundwork for radio transmission was laid in the nineteenth century and although early wireless and crystal sets were in use soon after 1900, the modern radio did not appear until after the First World War.

Some collectors are interested in the wireless and crystal sets, but because these look more like scientific instruments than what most people think of as radios, they are not generally popular. It was only with the coming of commercial radio stations (Pittsburgh's KDKA was the first) in 1920 that the public at large had a reason to own a set. Once this happened there was a substantial demand for reasonably attractive radios that would fit into the living room as well as the workshop.

Manufacturers such as Atwater-Kent, Magnavox, Zenith, RCA, and Radiola responded with a variety of receivers. In the early 1920s these were battery powered and equipped with earphones or large wooden or hard-rubber speakers similar to those on vintage victrolas. But the consumers were not happy with battery-operated radios. The battery acid was corrosive, and the batteries had to be recharged.

By 1927 manufacturers had solved the problem with the introduction of tube sets, which could be plugged into an AC electric socket. At first these were table models, but by 1929 many companies were making console radios that were built into furniture cases so that they could blend easily with the living room furniture. Well-constructed consoles were the centerpieces of many homes until they were replaced, after the Second World War, by the hi-fi set and the television.

Although consoles are popular with many collectors, their size usually limits the number that can be owned. Table models, on the other hand, come in various collectible sizes. Among the most popular are the smaller cabinet radios in the cathedral style, which were called midgets or depression models, the latter name because of their appearance during the hard times of the 1930s. Other interesting types are the Art Deco plastic table models, also from the 1930s, the early "portables" (some of which weighed forty pounds!), and automobile radios. As with phonographs, accessories and advertising materials associated with radios offer a fertile field for the collector.

Edison Standard phonograph; ca. 1905; $425–475.
This early phonograph utilized two- and four-inch wax
cylinders.

The Graphophone, Eagle model; by Columbia Phono- ▼
graph Co.; patented 1897; $350–425. This is an early
tin-horn phonograph.

The Gramaphone, model
Q; by Columbia
Phonograph Co.; patented
1898; $225–260. Note the
wax cylinder in place on
this phonograph.

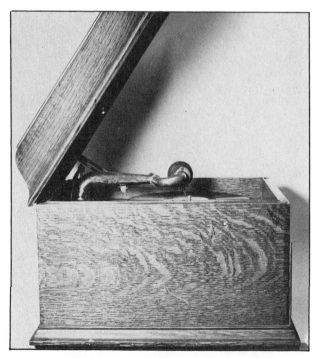

Victrola, model V-VII; by Victor Talking Machine;
1915–20; $200–275.

Arionola; by Arion Manufacturing Co.; ca. 1923; $250–300.

Early phonograph horns. *Above:* Brown papier-mache megaphone type; 1890–1900; $70–95. *Below:* Tin "morning glory" in blue, pink, and gold; 1880–90; $100–125.

Victor Talking Machine; model VV-VI; by Victor Talking Machine; 1918–22; $170–195.

Edison Tin Triumph phonograph horn; 1900–05; $120–145. An eleven-panel horn with collapsible stand.

Victrola, standard model A, with red metal horn; by Columbia Phonograph Co.; ca. 1901; $550–750. An uncommon early disc victrola in excellent condition.

Edison floor model victrola in oak cabinet; 1915–25; $245–285.

Edison Diamond Disc floor model phonograph in mahogany veneer case; 1920–30; $400–550.

Philco combination radio-phonograph in wood and plastic; ca. 1946; $125–175.

Edison wax phonograph cylinders; 1898–1910. *Left:* Gold Moulded; $8–14. *Center:* Amberol; $5–12. *Right:* Blue Amberol; $10–15.

Early 78 rpm phonograph records. *Left:* Edison Re-Creation; 1905–10; $5–10. *Right:* Little Wonder; patented 1909; $8–14. The Edison record is a "fat" record, over a quarter-inch thick.

Record jacket and 78 rpm records by jazz musician "Fats" Waller; 1935–40; $75–135. Records by popular artists always bring high prices.

33 rpm Picture Records; by Sav-Way Industries; ca. 1947; $75–115 for the album.

Wurlitzer jukebox, No. 1015, in plastic, chrome, and glass with oak veneer case; ca. 1946; $3,500–5,000. ▼

◀ Wurlitzer jukebox, No. 1080A, in plastic, chrome, and glass with oak veneer case; ca. 1947; $4,500–5,500.

Left: Willemin crystal set in metal and wood; 1923–25; $70–95. *Center* and *right:* Philmore crystal set in brown Bakelite with original box; 1935–40; $35–55.

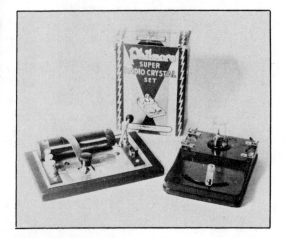

Left: Portable Opera crystal set; by Superior Products; ca. 1925; $100–135. *Right:* All metal crystal set; ca. 1928; $125–150. ▼

Ozarka radio receiver with pot-metal speaker, by Algonquin; ca. 1926; $225–275.

Reflect Type D-10 radio receiver with aerial; by De Forest; 1923–24; $600–750. This battery-powered radio is by one of the earliest radio manufacturers.

Interior view of a Montroset AM radio receiver, showing early tubes; ca. 1925; $110–140.

AM radio receiver by Freed-Eisemann; ca. 1924; $155–180.

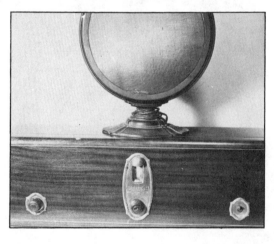

RCA Radiola receiver and speaker in mahogany case; ca. 1928; $180–225. This is one of the first radios that could be plugged into a wall outlet.

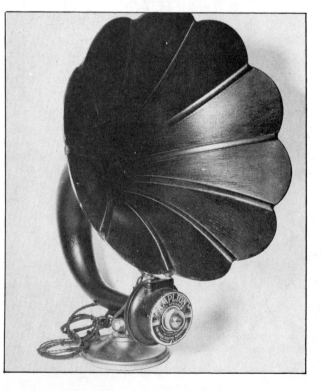

Amplon radio speaker in metal and wood; by Signal Electric; 1922–26; $150–185.

Pathe cone-type radio speaker in bronzed pot metal; ca. 1924; $115–145.

Cathedral-style table radio; by General Electric; ca. 1933; $165–205. The wooden cathedral- or Gothic-style radio was popular throughout the 1930s.

Philco Junior cathedral-style radio in light and dark wood; ca. 1932; $115–145. A typical "poor man's" radio of the early 1930s.

Monarch table radio in walnut veneer; ca. 1936; $140–175.

Art Deco table radio in oak veneer; by Sparton; 1933–35; $120–150. Nearly all wooden table radios were finished in shades of brown.

Philco Baby Grand cathedral-style radio; ca. 1931; $175–200.

Crosley Playtime radio in case of brown molded composition material; ca. 1930; $150–185. This early table radio is in the Art Nouveau mode.

Philco table radio in light and dark wood veneer; ca. 1934; $95–120.

Art Deco five-band radio; by Zenith; ca. 1935; $180–210.

Philco Art Deco table model radio in brown wood finish; ca. 1937; $85–125.

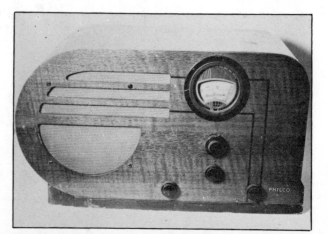

Emerson table radio in brown plastic; 1935–40; $65–100. Art Deco styled plastic radios are now in great demand.

RCA Victor table radio in cream-colored plastic; 1940–45; $75–120.

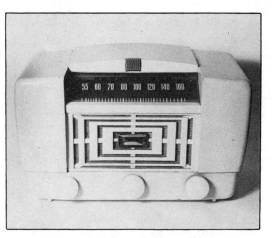

Art Deco table radio in blue glass and chrome; by Sparton; 1935–40; $225–275. A relatively uncommon and very stylish type.

RCA Victor radio in red Catalin; ca. 1940; $150–200. Catalin was a forerunner of modern plastic.

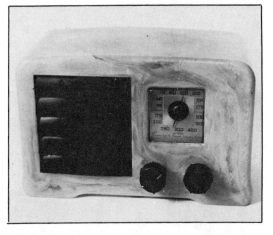

Small table radio in black and yellow plastic; by Emerson; 1940-45; $115–165.

RCA Victor table radio in orange and purple Catalin; 1940–45; $135–185.

Unusual Art Deco chairside model radio; 1940–45; $200–275.

Radiobar, combination floor model radio and bar; by Philco; ca. 1933; $400–550. An unusual and choice example.

Radio built into Tudor-style occasional table; by Atwater Kent; ca. 1929; $275–350.

Refrigerator-top radio in gold and cream; by Westinghouse; 1935–40; $65–90. These radios were made in colors to match various Westinghouse refrigerators.

Radio built into jewelry case; by Emerson; ca. 1946; $65–90. This is one of many novelty radios produced during the 1930s and 1940s.

Radio built into black-rubber miniature of General Tire; 1945–50; $140–190. Probably an advertising item.

The Country Belle, radio built into oak wall telephone case; 1940–50; $225–275.

Radio designed to resemble a book; by Sentinel; 1940–50; $75–105.

Radio in the form of a radio broadcasting mike; ca. 1935; $115–145.

Salesman's sample of console-type floor standing radio; 1933–35; $100–140. Though not a true radio, the piece could accommodate a speaker attached to a radio.

Radio broadcasting mike in the form of a telephone speaker; 1920–25; $100–135.

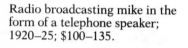

Radio related accessories. *Left:* Radio receiver's log housed in miniature tin box in the form of a radio; ca. 1930; $35–50. *Center:* Radio Tube Trick puzzle; 1935–40; $15–25. *Right:* Lilliputian Wireless toy; 1925–30; $20–30.

Magazines devoted to radio. *Left: Radio News;* April, 1929; $5–8. *Center: QST, Amateur Radio;* 1924; $8–11. *Right: Radio Guide;* October, 1937; $6–9.

Black pot-metal ashtray produced for RCA World Wide Wireless; 1920–25; $35–55.

Set of metal chimes awarded by NBC to every salesman selling over $1 million in advertising; 1930–40; $200–260.

Coca-Cola advertising sign promoting Edgar Bergen and Charlie McCarthy; 1940–45; $115–165.

Papier-mache figure of Nipper, the RCA Victor advertising dog; 1940–45; $750–950.

Enamel on tin advertising sign for Radiola Dealer; 1930–35; $150–200.

Militaria

Considering the horrors of war, it may seem surprising that there is any interest in the objects associated with it, but militaria has been collected for centuries. Moreover, the abundance of material left over from the First and Second World Wars has led to a greatly increased number of collectors.

Collectible military objects range from such obvious choices as guns and edged weapons to uniforms, medals, and even paper memorabilia such as recruiting posters and handwritten officer's commissions. Much of this material is American, but much is not, and most collectors are interested in foreign items. Those collectors who concentrate on the world wars seek equipment used by all the participants, with German and Japanese items being particularly favored.

Weapons are, of course, one of the most popular areas of militaria. However, they present certain problems for the collector. All cartridge-firing (as opposed to flint- or matchlock) rifles and handguns—which means essentially all post-1880 examples—are subject to state or local licensing. They are regarded as dangerous weapons, and they cannot be owned legally without being registered. As a consequence, many enthusiasts restrict their collecting to earlier or clearly inoperable types of firearms. Edged weapons, such as swords and daggers, while not usually subject to such regulations, can also pose a problem. Not only are they dangerous, but they are also salable; security for a collection of edged weapons is very important.

Though the United States was relatively late developing an efficient military rifle, weapons made by such firms as Springfield and Remington were issued in vast numbers between 1880 and 1940 and are still relatively common. Particularly desirable are the short-barreled carbines used by cavalrymen. It was, however, in the area of handguns that American manufacturers excelled, pioneering development of multiple-shot revolvers such as the Remington .44 and the single-action Colt as well as the famous Colt .45 automatic, which was adopted by the U.S. Army in 1911.

Edged weapons are also of interest to collectors. By the 1880s, the only American military men carrying swords were officers and some cavalrymen, but quite a few of their curved sabers can still be obtained. Bayonets, which have been used since the seventeenth century, are even more common. They range in length from seven to thirty inches, with the earlier, triangular examples considered most desirable. Other cutting tools include machetes of various sorts and the short knives used by rangers and other special forces.

Uniforms are another important area of militaria. The collector can concentrate on the colorful dress uniforms worn by state militia units and by the regular armed forces during the nineteenth century, or the collector can seek out the more available, if less attractive, standard issue garb of the post-1900 era. Dress uniforms were elaborately cut, brightly colored, and festooned with gold braid. They reflect an era when a uniform was often a matter of personal preference and camouflage was yet unknown. The more practical khaki or olive-drab breeches and tunic or jacket became standard issue for the U.S. Army in 1902 and, along with air force and navy uniforms from the two world wars, are readily available.

Military caps, hats, and helmets are both extremely interesting and easy to store. They are found in great variety, reflecting the many changes in military fashions over the past century. For years after the Civil War most American troops wore the kepi, a soft-sided, low-crowned cap. Some units wore the European shako, a spectacular-looking hat in the form of a tall leather cylinder surmounted by a colorful plume. Though abandoned by the regular military soon after 1900, the shako continued to be favored by state militias, particularly as parade garb. The beret, which is widely worn today, was not introduced until 1916, when it was issued for the convenience of tank crews. For many years most American soldiers wore the high-crowned, wide-brimmed hat now associated with the Boy Scouts.

Steel helmets are of no great antiquity. Body armor was abandoned shortly after the introduction of firearms, and it was not until the First World War that helmets once more appeared on the battlefield. Most helmets were roughly pot-shaped, such as the British helmet that was used by the U.S. Army until 1942. Of more interest are unusual types such as the German Stahlhelm and the crested helmet of the French soldiers. Helmets are relatively inexpensive and easy to find.

For the collector who wants something a bit smaller than helmets, there are medals. Medals can be divided into two general categories: campaign medals issued to troops who served in a certain battle or area of operations, and awards for valor, such as the American Distinguished Service Cross, first issued in 1918. Most campaign medals of the post-1900 period were issued in great quantity and are quite inexpensive. Certain awards of valor, on the other hand, are quite rare and command a high price. This has led, unfortunately, to reproductions. There are, for example, more fake Medals of Honor circulating today than there are legitimately issued medals. Since medals are so available and so widely collected, they are graded as to quality much like old coins. Gradations run from excellent (FDC) through very fine (VF) and fine (F) to fair and worn.

There are a great many other military collectibles. Objects available range all the way from the popular brass belt buckles and uniform buttons to such mundane things as trench shovels, canteens, and various bullets and projectiles. Militaria is a wide field, with many specialized areas.

U.S. Army Remington "rolling block" system cavalry carbine, .44 caliber; 1890–95; $150–210.

Pair of revolvers; by Remington Arms Co. *Top:* Percussion type; 1870–80; $115-145. *Bottom:* Percussion type modified to rim fire; 1880–90; $165–225.

U.S. Army model 1873 Springfield training rifle; dated 1881; $75–100.

U.S. Army Remington percussion-type revolver, .44 caliber; 1865–80; $175–235.

273

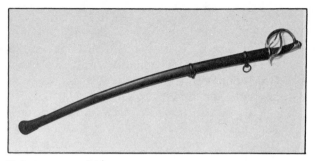

U.S. Army model 1860 calavry saber,
brass and steel; 1880–90; $125–170.

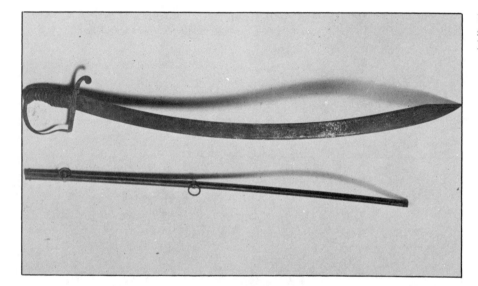

U.S. Army cavalry saber, iron and
steel; by W. Rose Co.; Philadelphia,
Pa.; 1870–80; $240–330.

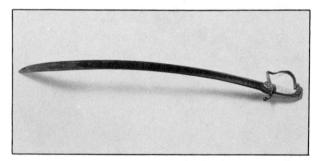

American officer's dress sword, ivory,
iron, and steel; 1910–20; $175–250.

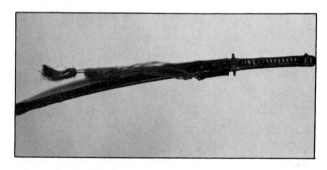

Japanese officer's samurai sword, iron,
steel, and brass; 1935–45; $225–300.

Japanese officer's samurai sword, iron
and steel; 1935–45; $175–250. Swords
such as this were popular G.I. souvenirs.

U.S. Army bayonets, iron and steel; by Remington
Arms Co.; 1915–20; $20–35 each.

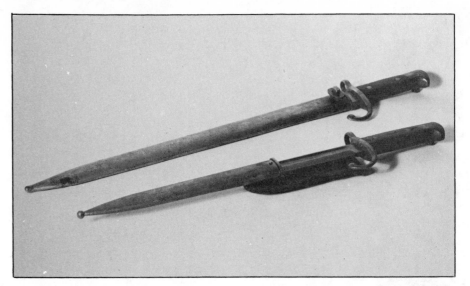

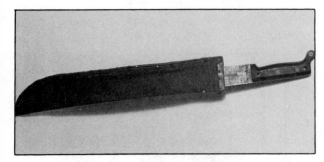

U.S. Army machete, steel and horn; by Ontario Knife
Co.; dated 1943; $15–25.

Complete dress or parade
uniform, Seventh Regiment, New
York National Guard; 1870–80;
$350–425.

American hospital corpsman's knife, steel and wood;
1905–10; $95–130. Knives of this sort were issued for
use during the Philippine insurrection. A very rare
piece.

Dress blue jacket, Vermont Militia;
1880–90; $85–145.

U.S. Navy officer's jacket in dark blue wool; 1914–18; $55–80.

U.S. Army uniform jacket in khaki wool; 1914–18; $25–45.

U.S. Army officer's jacket in khaki wool; 1914–18; $40–70.

U.S. Air Force uniform coat and shirt in blue wool; 1942–46; $25–40.

U.S. Army uniform jacket in khaki wool; 1942–46; $20–30. Note that the buttons have been replaced.

U.S. Army fatigue caps. *Left:* Kepi in blue wool; 1880–90; $125–165. *Right:* Standard undress cap, Twenty-fifth Infantry; 1890–95; $60–85.

New York State Militia shako, black felt, leather, and gold braid; 1880–1910; $135–185.

U.S. Army officer's cap in khaki; 1914–18; $35–55.

West Point Military Academy shako, brass and black leather; 1890–1900; $125–170.

French Army kepi in black leather and red felt; 1914–18; $300–400.

Austrian kepi in black leather, gold braid, and brass fittings; 1914–18; $310–380.

French military school kepi in blue and black leather with brass fittings; 1915–20; $275–375.

French grenadier's bearskin hat in leather and black bear fur with brass fittings; 1870–80; $145–190.

Australian field hat in khaki felt with feathers and red cotton band; 1940–45; $85–115. Aussie troops made these hats famous throughout the Pacific.

British pith helmet covered in sand-color cotton; 1940–45; $120–165.

German pith helmet, Afrika Corps; 1939–45; $90–135.

German steel helmet, or Stahlhelm, in camouflage colors; 1914–18; $65–90.

German steel helmet liner with extended neck piece; 1914–18; $40–55. The neck piece was designed to provide further protection against shrapnel from shells bursting above the trenches.

U.S. campaign medals in brass; 1941–45; $8–15 each.

U.S. campaign medals; 1941–45; $10–17 each. Medals such as these provide an inexpensive start for a collection.

Gambling Devices

Americans are probably the world's greatest gamblers, with fully 70 percent of our population gambling on something at one time or another each year. For many people it is horse racing or the World Series or a big college football game, but for others only the lure of organized gambling will suffice. A great variety of devices, from the roulette wheel and slot machine to the bingo card, has been devised to satisfy this urge, and all the items are collectible.

The greatest range of collector interest centers on the arcade (from penny arcade, of course) games that first appeared in the late nineteenth century. Many of these were not truly gambling games at all, though they were designed to take the customer's money. Devices such as weight lifters, grip testers, and automatic fortune tellers offered a service, albeit a dubious one: They could "predict" the future or help a boy to convince his girl that he was a strongman. But they couldn't double your money, and that was what the public really wanted.

It wasn't long before that desire was satisfied. Soon after 1900, Herbert S. Mills, a Chicago arcade owner, developed the Mills Dewey, a metal box with a color-coded interior wheel activated by a hand crank. The player put his nickel into one of six similarly color-coded slots, spun the handle, and if the color that came up on the wheel matched that of his slot, he collected a handful of coins. Even if he didn't win, the player got to listen to a tune played on the music box built into the machine.

The Mills creation was soon improved upon by Charles Fey of San Francisco, who invented the first true slot machine, the Liberty Bell. The Bell differed from the Dewey by having three independently revolving wheels that had to line up in a predetermined sequence in order to produce a winning combination. Though Fey's device used playing card suits rather than the now familiar plums, oranges, and lemons, it was the prototype of the modern "one-arm bandit."

Mills marketed a pirated version of the un-patented Fey slot machine in 1907, and in 1925 he added the jackpot device to further stimulate play. By that time, slot machines had swept the country and could be found in penny arcades, country stores, and even post offices. But with the coming of the Great Depression, the powers that be decided the people should put what little money they had to some better use. By the end of the 1930s, slot machines had been outlawed in nearly every state.

But the interest never died, and throughout the country there are collectors seeking the machines. Among the brands in greatest demand are Rock-Ola, Evans, Pace, and Jennings. Some of these products are floor standing, but the majority are designed to sit atop a stand or table. As a general rule, the earlier the slot machine, the more desirable it is, though some collectors seek out the most complex or most visually attractive examples.

As the pressure against gambling mounted, many manufacturers came out with machines that paid off in candy, cigarettes, or even golf balls—anything that wasn't money but would still offer an inducement to put the nickel in the slot. These later machines are collectible, and in some cases they are less common than their money-spitting brethren.

The roulette wheel is another very collectible gambling tool. This enameled metal wheel may be set spinning manually or automatically, causing a ball to roll around suspensefully and eventually settle in one of several numbered slots. Bettors gamble on where the ball will end up. Though hardly a complex game, roulette is a very popular one. It was played in Europe and America during the mid-nineteenth century and continues to attract crowds wherever gambling is tolerated. The larger wheels were built into tables specially designed for use in casinos, and these machines are usually difficult to obtain. More readily available are the miniature versions intended for home use. Collectors are also interested in the colorful "layouts," in wood or cloth, which were used with roulette or various card and dice games. Layouts were the temporary surfaces on which the game was played, and many early examples were hand painted.

For the many gamblers who couldn't afford roulette, there was always bingo, a slightly more complicated version of the Italian parlor game lotto, which was popular in New Orleans as early as 1840. Bingo has long been legal in many states, and is a major source of funding for many church groups. Bingo collectibles include scorecards, markers, numbered wooden or plastic balls, and the large wire cages in which the balls were stirred up and from which they were drawn.

Similar in principle to roulette are the many different "side games" popular at casinos, amusement parks, and carnivals. These usually are based on a revolving wheel, with players betting on which number the wheel will stop at when spun by the operator. Like most "carny" games, money wheels are usually fixed in favor of the house.

Gamblers seeking entertainment involving more skill and less luck could pitch pennies (the collectibles here are the brightly painted boards on which the coins fell) or play one of several versions of the knockdown game. The latter involved either throwing a ball through a small hole in a screen or using it to try to knock over milk-bottle-shaped figures. The painted canvas screens are collectible, and the weighted figures, often colored to look like clowns, are also desirable.

For the gambler's more quiet hours there were the punchboards that once graced nearly every saloon and corner grocery. Punchboards, which were outlawed in the late 1940s, are very simple in concept. Tiny slips of paper imprinted with numbers or names are inserted in holes drilled in a large piece of cardboard. The player pays a nickel or so for a chance to poke out one of the slips. The name or number on the slip is then checked against a master list to see if the player wins a prize—usually a piece of merchandise, though sometimes money was offered.

Punchboards were designed to attract customers, particularly men, and many featured brightly colored versions of latter-day Gibson girls as well as exaggerated descriptions of prizes to be won. Today, unused punchboards and associated advertising materials are hard to come by and can bring high prices.

Punchboards, of course, were often rigged in favor of the seller, just as most gambling devices were rigged in favor of the casino or the professional gambler. In fact, some of the most interesting gambling accessories are the instruments used to cheat. There are machines to shave the edges of cards; "hold outs," which pop the right card into the gambler's hand at the right moment; and many different sorts of rigged dice and card dispensers. All are highly collectible, but none are easy to acquire. Some, no doubt, are still in use!

Other collectible gambling devices include playing cards (an entire field in themselves), lottery tickets, admission stubs to horse races and other sporting events, and bone or plastic dice.

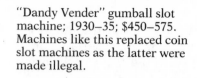

"Dandy Vender" gumball slot machine; 1930–35; $450–575. Machines like this replaced coin slot machines as the latter were made illegal.

HiTop 7-7-7 quarter-play slot machine; by Mills; 1930–40; $750–950. Although outlawed in most states, slot machines are among the most favored gambling collectibles.

Tavern gumball slot machine; 1930–40; $425–525.

Win a Beer tavern gambling game; 1940–50; $250–325. A penny in the slot causes the dice to roll, and participants bet on their fall.

Casino-size (thirty inches in diameter) roulette wheel, inlaid and veneered in mahogany; 1890–1900; $3,000–4,000.

Traveling roulette wheel in black Bakelite with a green baize layout; 1930–40; $70–110. These sets were used in private homes as well as by professional gamblers.

Lithographed tin serving tray in the form of a roulette wheel; 1935–40; $70–85.

Small (fourteen inches in diameter) roulette wheel of ebonized wood and chrome; 1900–10; $250–340. For home use by professional gamblers.

Left: Ivory roulette chips in red, green, tan, and white; 1900–10; $5–9 each. *Right:* Bakelite faro chips in purple, tan, and red; 1920–25; $3–6.

Roulette layout in red and black on gray felt; 1890–1900; $500–600. Layouts were the surface on which bets were placed in roulette and various dice or card games. Because of their fragile material, few have survived.

Large revolving wooden dice bowl; 1870–80; $900–1,400. This device was called a Hyronemus Tub, and the dice employed with it were two inches wide.

Casino-type dice cage of nickel-plated brass; ca. 1920; $250–300.

One-foot-high home dice cage; 1930–40; $70–95. Though intended to prevent cheating, dice cages could be fixed, usually through magnetic devices.

Bubble dice shaker with dice; 1920–30; $200–275. Next to the bubble is a magnet with which the gambler could control the fall of the dice.

Left: Wooden dice drop; 1870–80; $235–280. *Center:* Glass and wood dice drop; 1920–25; $160–195. *Right:* Wooden dice drop; 1880–90; $240–290.

Rear: Stamped-leather dice cup; 1900–10; $45–65. *Front:* Poker dice; 1900–05; $20–30.

Automatic draw poker dice box; patented 1890; $475–600. Pushing the rod at the end of the box makes the dice spin. The player can "hold" by pushing in one or more of the five rods in the side of the box.

Typical dice game layout in green and orange; by Field; ca. 1900; $400–550.

Poker chip holder of laminated wood; 1930–40; $35–45.

Casino card press used to keep playing cards in good condition; 1880–90; $325–350.

Left: Deck of faro cards; 1880–90; $120–150. *Right:* Dealer's box of German silver; 1885–95; $135–175. Dealer's boxes were intended to prevent unfair deals, but many, such as this one, were rigged in the dealer's favor.

Gaming kit of wood covered in mottled paper; 1870–80; $260–325. Used in playing whist, these boxes came equipped with whist cards and wood or bone markers.

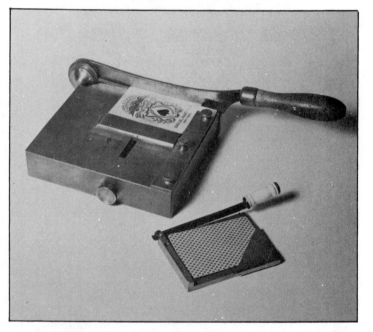

Wooden case used to keep track of cards played in a game of faro; by George Williams; New York, N.Y.; ca. 1870; $900–1,200. This box may be one of a kind.

Whist gaming kit in walnut and brass; 1860–70; $275–325.

Brass card trimmers; 1850–90. *Left:* Casino size; $1,600–2,200. *Right:* Tiny ivory-handled traveling card sharp's trimmer; 1,300–1,700. These devices were used to shave certain playing cards, making them distinguishable from the others in the deck.

Shears-type card trimmer of brass and steel; 1880–90; $1,650–2,250. Card trimmers are uncommon and expensive.

Corner trimmer of brass and iron; 1870–80; $1,800–2,300. Used to reshape the corners of playing cards after they had been trimmed.

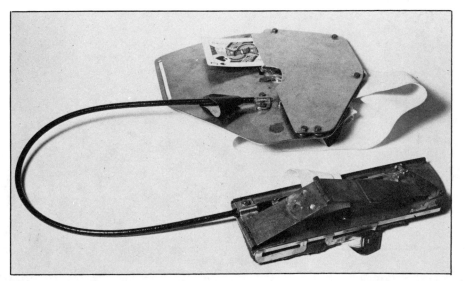

Vest-mounted gambler's "holdout"; 1900–10; $1,800–2,400. Operated by pressure on the spring device concealed behind the knee, the holdout would slip a wanted card into the gambler's hand.

Layout for high-low in red, black, and white on green baize; 1890–1900; $500–650.

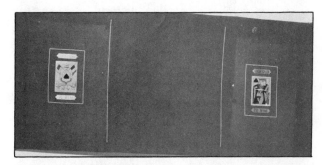

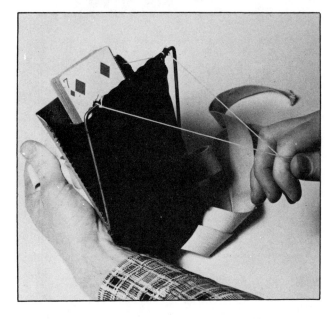

"Cold deck" machine of metal; ca. 1920; $1,500–2,100. Concealed on the card sharp's person, this handy device was used to produce a complete set of new cards in the course of a game.

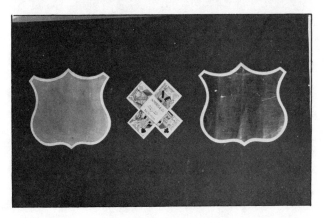

Layout in red and black on green for the game of red and black; by Harris & Co.; New York; N.Y.; $800–950.

Layout for chuck-a-luck in green and white on a black background; by H. C. Evans; Chicago, Ill.; 1880–1900; $500–625.

Bingo cage of metal and wood with Bakelite posts and handle; 1930–35; $70–105.

Layout for diana in wood and baize; by William Suydam; New York, N.Y.; 1870–80; $4,500–6,500. This is one of two known existing examples.

Gambling tops; 1880–1920. *Left:* Plastic for use in high-low; $20–28. *Center left:* Plastic for use in put and take; $15–25. *Center right:* Brass for use in horse race; $35–45. *Right:* Brass dice; $45–55.

Keno scorecards; by H. C. Evans; Chicago, Ill.; 1920–30; $5–8 each. Keno was an early form of bingo. form of bingo.

Books on card playing. *Left: The Card Player;* 1870–80; $25–40. *Center: Card Sharpers;* ca. 1903; $45–60. *Right: Whist;* 1900–10; $10–15.

Pamphlets on gambling. *Left: The Thompson Street Poker Club;* 1888–90; $80–120. *Right: Why Gamblers Win;* ca. 1900; $40–60.

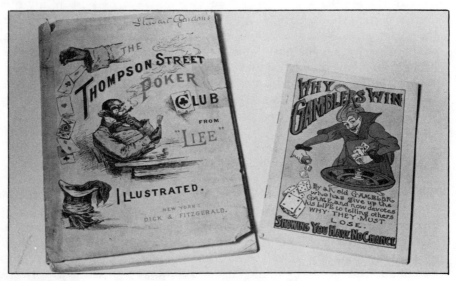

Chalkware tobacco humidor in blue, cream, and tan; 1900–10; $250–300.

Lithographed print of dogs gambling; 1910–20; $35–45.

Games

Toys and dolls have been widely collected in the United States for decades. Prices for most items are high, and competition among collectors is fierce. However, one related area has been left relatively untouched: games.

As long as people have had leisure, they have had games with which to pass the time. Backgammon, a current craze, was known in the seventeenth century, and dice and playing cards go back to the Middle Ages. The era with which we are concerned, however, saw the culmination of the parlor game. With the increased free time that the prosperity of the late nineteenth century brought to an expanding middle class and the invention of electric lighting—which made it possible for the first time to comfortably perform activities at night—the public clamored for amusements.

One of the most popular of these amusements was checkers, and the number of paintings and lithographs depicting checker players sitting on the porch or around the old potbellied stove is mute evidence of the popularity of this pastime among our ancestors. Many commercial manufacturers produced checkerboards, but the boards most interesting to today's collectors are the handmade versions of light and dark wood inlaid in a contrasting pattern or painted in bright hues. The most interesting of these boards can be viewed as a form of folk art, and many today are collected as such. Much the same can be said of backgammon and Parcheesi boards, some of which were made of glass with the board design painted in reverse on the back of the glass.

There are also the counters with which the games were played. Checkers, being only plain circles of wood, are of little interest, but chessmen have been made of everything from wood to precious metals, and they are collected with great enthusiasm.

The greatest variety of games is found among those played upon a board, and these are, appropriately, known to collectors as board games.

Most board games are similar in concept, involving a race to the finish line between two or more players who move their pieces, or counters, along a printed track at a rate determined by the fall of dice, the turn of a numbered spinner, or the selection of cards.

The earliest known board game, Goose, was played in Italy in the sixteenth century, but it was not until the 1800s that such recreational devices existed in any quantity. Yet from about 1870 to the 1960s, when television began to affect their popularity, thousands of such games were put on the market. Some never caught the public fancy and were soon discontinued, while others enjoyed phenomenal success. The Mansion of Happiness, a game with a religious theme, was first marketed in 1843 and was still being reissued as late as the 1880s. That is nothing compared to everyone's favorite, Monopoly. Though a relative latecomer (it was invented in 1935) compared to such games as Lotto, Old Maid, and even bingo, Monopoly has already sold over 80 million sets! The story is that its creator, Charles Darrow, was broke and out of work when he came up with this bright idea, and he made enough money from it to indulge his own interests in real estate speculation as well as to become a world traveler and orchid grower.

Games collectors are always interested in the themes of their acquisitions and how they are played, but the main reason that most people collect is that they are attracted by the lovely graphics with which the boards and particularly the box covers are adorned. Early examples were lithographed in black on white and then carefully hand tinted, but by the 1880s, chromolithography had made possible multicolored designs. Some of these are faithful reproductions of Victorian dress and customs, and others are strikingly abstract. In either case the cover is the object of greatest importance. If it is lost or damaged, few collectors are interested in the game. The absence of markers, cards, or spinners is not critical, though it detracts from the value of the set. The ideal acquisition, of course, is a game that is complete and in good condition.

Given the large number of games that have been produced, one would expect that the game collector would have little trouble acquiring specimens. However, since most games were made of cardboard and paper, time has taken its toll. All too many games have been either lost or damaged beyond repair. Fortunately, the field is relatively new, and serious collectors are few enough that good examples can still be obtained at reasonable prices. Knowledgeable dealers will charge thirty or forty dollars for a full-size game (about eighteen inches across), but similar games can be found at flea markets or even yard sales at a fraction of that price.

The observant collector soon realizes that the majority of games from the period from 1880 to 1950 were made by one of three companies. One of the earliest of these companies was the W. & S.B. Ives Company of Salem, Massachusetts. Ives developed the game with the longest name, Pope and Pagan, or The Missionary Compaign; or the Siege of the Stronghold of Satan by the Christian Army. Like many other late-nineteenth-century games, Pope and Pagan had a religious message to convey—other board games of the period were designed to teach geography or simple bookkeeping or to inculcate social values such as honesty and respect for hard work.

The other major board-game producers were McLoughlin Brothers of New York City, active from 1850 until its absorption in 1920 by the Milton Bradley Company of Springfield, Massachusetts; and Parker Brothers, of Salem, Massachusetts, manufacturer of Monopoly.

Puzzles are also collectible. Wood or cardboard puzzles have been popular a long time—during the 1860s Milton Bradley made a puzzle called The Smashed Up Locomotive. Puzzles with unusual shapes or themes (such as animals or national maps) are considered the most desirable.

Building blocks—from the early ones that were made of wooden blocks to which lithographed paper was pasted to the modern plastic version—are considered highly collectible. Because age is very important with these, twentieth-century examples remain underpriced. As with board games and puzzles, original boxes in good condition are critical.

Game of Mail, Express or Accommodation; by Milton Bradley Co.; ca. 1923; ; $35–50. The fine lines and dynamic coloring of this board game's box top typify what collectors look for in this area.

Doodle-Bug Race; by Selchow and Righter; 1925–35; $40–50. So-called Mexican jumping beans are the counters in this unusual game.

Barney Google and Spark Plug Game; by Milton Bradley Co.; ca. 1923; $40–65. Many games are based on comic strip figures.

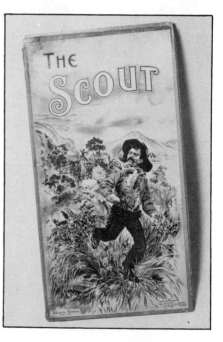

The Scout; by Edgar O. Clark; 1900–05; $30–45. Though based on an American theme, this game was manufactured in England.

African Hunter
Game; by Hoge
Manufacturing
Co.; 1935–45;
$30–45.

Board games; by Milton Bradley Co.; 1930–35; $25–40
each. *Top:* Fox and Geese. *Bottom:* Bang.

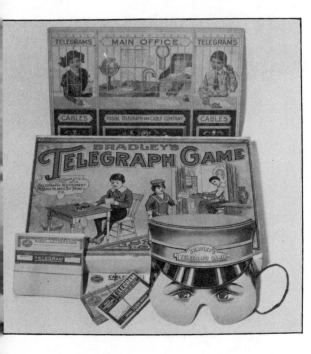

Toonin Radio
Game; by Alder-
mann, Fairchild
Co.; 1930–35;
$40–60. This game
reflects manufac-
turers' interest in
the booming
communications
industry.

Telegraph Game; by Milton Bradley Co.; 1920–25;
$55–75. Good lithography and no missing pieces make
this a most desirable game.

Game of the
Spider's Web; by
Milton Bradley
Co.; 1920–25;
$30–40.

The Gypsy Fortune Telling
Game; by Milton Bradley Co.;
1930–40; $30–45.

Conjuring Tricks; by Spears; 1930–35;
$30–45. Amateur magician sets have
been popular for a long time with both
children and adults.

The Hand of Fate Fortune Telling
Game; by McLoughlin Brothers; ca.
1901; $50–65.

Peg Baseball; by
Parker Brothers;
1915–20; $45–60.

Major League
Baseball Game;
ca. 1912; $75–100.
This early
baseball game is
highlighted by the
presence of Babe
Ruth—on the
Boston Braves!

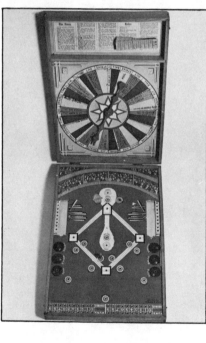

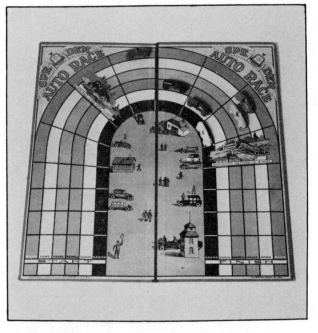

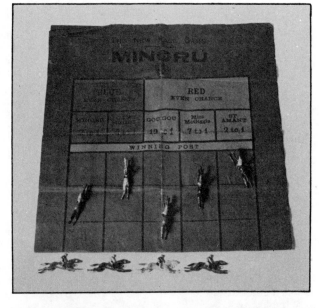

Minoru; by John Jacques & Sons; England; 1910–15; $100–140. Multicolored lead horses race on a green oilcloth course.

Spedem Auto Race; by Aldermann, Fairchild Co.; ca. 1922; $65–90. Unusual metal cars add much to this game.

Board games with religious themes; by Goodenough & Woglom; 1930–40; $5–15 each. *Top:* Bible Lotto. *Bottom:* Bible Quotto.

Glass and metal puzzles that involve rolling balls; 1925–35. *Left:* Baseball; $15–22. *Center:* Spider; $10–17. *Right:* Cootie Game; $18–28.

Handmade wooden checkerboard in pine with green and gray paint; 1890–1900; $130–175. Many checker- and chessboards were homemade.

Left: Checkers set and black and red checkerboard; by Embossing Co.; 1940–45; $10–20. *Right:* Parcheesi set; 1930–40; $15–25.

Checkers and backgammon board and box in the form of books; by McLoughlin Brothers; 1925–35; $20–35.

Board game; 1920–30; $40–55.

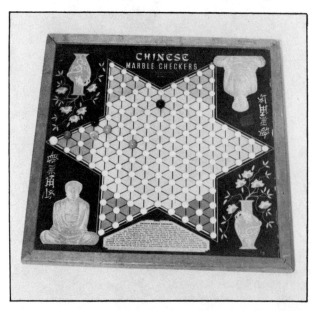

Dominoes in domino-shaped wooden box; 1030–35; $30–40. An unusual and well-designed set.

Chinese Marble Checkers; by Whitman Publishing Co.; ca. 1939; $15–25.

Ark dominoes; by Wilder
Manufacturing Co.; 1940–50;
$22–32.

Card games;
1925–35. *Left:*
Snap; by Milton
Bradley Co.; $10–
15. *Right:*
Touring; by Parker
Brothers; $12–18.
Bottom: Dr.
Busby; by Milton
Bradley Co.; $8–
13.

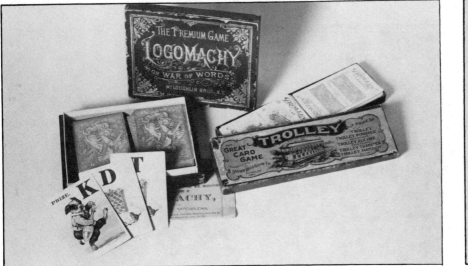

Left: LogoMachy;
by McLouglin
Brothers; ca. 1889;
$10–17. *Right:*
Trolley; by Snyder
Brothers Co.;
1910–20; $15–23.

Lost Heir; by
Milton Bradley
Co.; ca. 1908; $16–
24.

Left: Have U It; by
Selchow and
Righter; 1930–35;
$18–27. *Right top:*
Lindy; by Parker
Brothers; 1925–
30; $20–30. *Right
bottom:* Stock
Exchange; by W.
W. Gavitt Co.; ca.
1903; $5–10.

Top: Tiddledy Winks and Tiddledy Tots; by Transogram; 1935–45; $10–18. *Bottom:* Tiddledy Winks; by Parker Brothers; 1900–10; $9–16.

Left: Magnetic Jack Straws; by Milton Bradley Co.; 1920–25; $8–15. *Right:* Jack Straws by Milton Bradley Co.; 1930–35; $10–17.

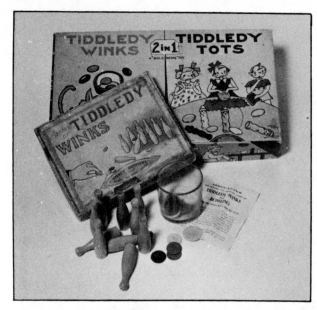

Magnetic Fish Pond; 1935–40; $30–45. The brightly colored fish are particularly well done.

Table Croquet; 1910–15; $25–40.

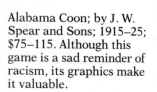

Alabama Coon; by J. W. Spear and Sons; 1915–25; $75–115. Although this game is a sad reminder of racism, its graphics make it valuable.

Pitch Em The Game of Indoor Horseshoes; by Walbert Manufacturing Co.; 1925–30; $15–25.

Jumpy Tinker; by Toy Tinkers Inc.;
1930–35; $27–38. "The sport that
keeps us young."

Tinkle Target; by Milton Bradley
Co.; 1890–1900; $50–70. When a
thrown ball hits the cat's head, a
bell rings.

Educational games that promote
wise spending; by Parker Brothers. *Left:* My Mother Sent Me to
the Grocery Store; 1910–20;
$15–24. *Right:* Corner Grocery;
ca. 1887; $25–38.

North Atlantic Squadron Picture
Puzzle; 1910–20; $150–175. A rare
picture puzzle with great graphics.

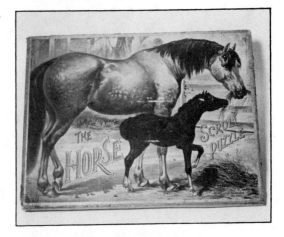

The Horse Scroll Puzzle; by
McLoughlin Brothers; ca. 1898;
$90–115.

"Favorite" Picture Puzzles; by Madmar Quality Co.; 1920–30; $45-65.

Storming of Weissenburg puzzle blocks; Germany; ca. 1872; $225–275. Extremely rare.

Block puzzle; 1910–20; $75–120. Because portions of a different puzzle are glued to each side of the wooden blocks, this set can produce six completely different puzzles.

Building blocks; by Richter & Co.; 1900–10; $110–165. Sets of these unusual blocks are rarely found intact.

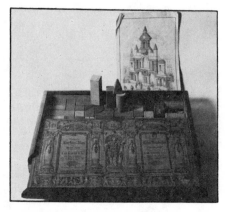

Block puzzle; 1890–1900; $70–110.

Cardboard puzzle blocks; 1915–25; $65–90.

Wooden building blocks in unpainted pine; 1900–10; $30–48.

Educational puzzle; by C. H. Stoelting Co.; 1945–55; $25–40.

Put a Hat on Uncle Wiggily pinup game; by Milton Bradley Co.; ca. 1919; $25–38.

Pat and His Pipe pinup game; 1930–35; $40–55.

Goof Race and Ten Pins; by Russell Manufacturing Co.; 1930–40; $25–37.

Soldiers on Parade, including fifty cardboard soldiers; by McLoughlin Brothers; ca. 1898; $175–245. Soldiers of all kinds are in great demand.

Tomorrow's Collectibles

Most collectors are good-natured people, happy with what they have and looking forward to acquiring more of the same. There are, however, always a few prophesiers of "doom and gloom" who declare that there is nothing left to collect and that all the good stuff is gone. They were saying that way back in the 1920s, and they are saying it today, but it is not true at all. We live in a world full of potential collectibles. Many of the things pictured and described in this book were not regarded as worthy of being collected twenty or thirty years ago, but today these items often bring higher prices than those paid for older antiques.

And there is more to come. As we move into the 1980s, more and more of the objects made during the 1960s and 1970s will be recognized as desirable collectibles. Which ones you will choose to collect will be largely a reflection of your interests and your pocketbook, but there are a few categories to keep in mind.

Contemporary craftsmen are creating some of the finest art pottery and art glass ever produced. Well trained and blessed with the advantages of modern technology, they are turning out a whole raft of fine things, from stoneware to sophisticated paperweights. A visit to one of the many local craft fairs or to a shop specializing in contemporary crafts should convince you that here may be found the Rookwood or Lalique of tomorrow. Buy it today!

There are also limited editions. These can be plates, pottery figurines, or silverware—often of a commemorative nature—which are made in a limited number and offered to the public with the inducement that over time they will appreciate in value. There is no doubt that limited editions can be both fun to collect and profitable. For instance, most of the Royal Copenhagen Christmas plates are now worth many times their original cost. On the other hand, with the large number of such

items on the market, it behooves the collector to buy carefully. Just how limited is the edition? An edition "limited" to 150,000 copies will probably take a long time to appreciate. And equally important is the quality of the pieces. Is the piece a good example of its type? An unattractive or poorly made plate or figure will probably never be in much demand, even if only a limited number are made.

But you really don't have to think only of investment when you buy. There are a lot of things passing through our hands every day that will, in time, be collectible. Many types of containers are gradually being phased out. The glass milk bottle is already gone; metal containers, such as tobacco tins, are slowly disappearing. As these are replaced by plastic, the remaining examples will attract great interest, particularly from those collectors interested in advertiques. While it may be argued that contemporary tins, boxes, and bottles lack the spectacular graphics of some late-nineteenth- and early-twentieth-century examples, it cannot be denied that some are very good indeed. Beer bottles provide an example. There is already an active group of collectors seeking contemporary specimens in this field. The short-lived Billy Beer is just one example of the available beer collectibles.

Nor is it a good idea to overlook plastics. Modern molded-plastic furniture is often both attractive and relatively inexpensive. There is little doubt that it will someday be as popular with furniture collectors and decorators as Art Deco furnishings are today. Much the same may be said of the tubular metal furniture that is also seen in so many homes and offices.

For those who want to own something a bit smaller and easier to store, there is a plethora of advertising paper, ranging from wall posters, signs, and leaflets to admission tickets and business cards. Now is the time to gather them while they are available and often being thrown away in large quantities. Keep an eye out for material relating to important events: political rallies, concerts (Beatle posters and other "Beatlemania" are already getting expensive), movies, and sporting events. Don't forget baseball, football, and hockey cards and admission tickets. Super Bowl tickets, for example, are highly collectible.

These are, of course, just a few of the many possibilities. There is no way to determine what will become tomorrow's one-of-a-kind collectible. Cigar bands? boxes? Or perhaps automobile collectibles, such as hubcaps and hood ornaments?

What about souvenirs? There are souvenir ashtrays, cups and saucers, postcards, and paper placemats. Comic books? Buttons? Already of interest to the Disco set are gas-station shirts and hats with advertising logos. Perhaps tin made-in-Japan robots will command high prices ten years from now. The collector of the future lets nothing worthwhile escape. He or she looks for good design and construction and that appealing "something" that makes a collectible collectible. There are thousands of items in our daily lives that meet these standards. Just choose the ones you prefer and don't worry because they aren't old. Like all of us, they will get there!

Clockwork windup toys; 1945–50; $8–15 each. *Left:* Occupied Japan. *Right:* U.S. Zone of West Germany.

Prices cannot yet be determined for most of the items illustrated in this chapter.

Miniatures in cast metal and plastic; 1970–75. *Left:* Harvester; by Lesney. *Center:* Racing car; by Polistill. *Right:* Ambulance; by Corgi. High-quality miniatures such as these are a fertile field for collectors.

Semimechanical figures of cast iron; Japan; 1976–78. Newly released "monster" figures such as these have attracted the eyes of children and collectors alike.

Earthenware tea set in green and cream glaze; by Carlee Weston; New York, N.Y.; 1979. The high quality of Ms. Weston's work is typical of modern art pottery.

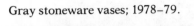
Red earthenware vase with copper highlights; 1978–79.

Gray stoneware vases; 1978–79.

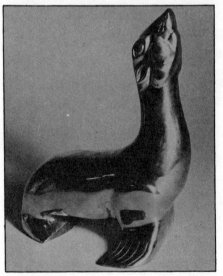

Brass seal; by Ethan Allen furniture; 1975–79. A good example of well-formed commercial sculpture.

Billy Beer can in aluminum; 1977–78. Beer cans are extremely popular, and the political associations of this one make it a sure bet for future collectors.

Seltzer-water bottle in green glass and metal; by Schrager's; New York, N.Y.; 1965–70. Color and form make seltzer bottles popular.

Political buttons in plastic and metal; 1960–70.

Beatles bubble-gum card in black and white; 1965–70. Beatlemania has brought about a boom in the price of related items.

45 rpm records; by the Beatles; 1963–66. Hard-to-find discs and first releases are already selling for as much as $50 each.

Limited-release 45 rpm record; by Patti Smith; 1974. Limited releases are always scarce and in demand.

Ashtray in yellow and white glaze; early 1970s. This smile motif was very popular.

Belt buckle of wrought brass and silver with inset agate; 1973. Craft objects like this have definite collector potential. This buckle was made by an inmate of the Wyoming State Penitentiary.

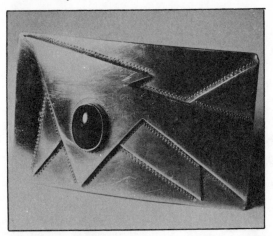

Miniature souvenir dishes from Washington, D.C., Niagara Falls, and Las Vegas; 1965–75. Popular pottery such as this can be inexpensively purchased today; tomorrow it will be at a premium.

Playbill for the Broadway comedy-melodrama revival of *Dracula*; 1978. Stage, screen, and radio memorabilia provide a fascinating field for the collector.

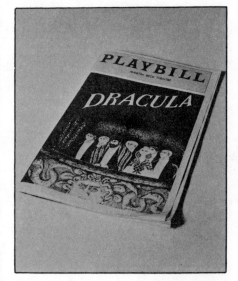

Miniature souvenir saucer and mug from St. Louis, Missouri; 1978–79.

Super Bowl ticket; 1978. World Series, Super Bowl, and N.B.A. basketball playoff tickets are attracting substantial collector interest.

Three early issues of *Famous Monsters of Filmland;* 1958–61.

Limited-edition hand-painted collector's plate in porcelain; by Knowles China Co.; dated 1978. Norman Rockwell design makes this a likely candidate for increased value.

Bibliography

Furniture

Clark, Robert J. *The Arts and Crafts Movement in America, 1876–1916.* Princeton, N.J.: Princeton University Press, 1972.

Hill, Conover. *Antique Oak Furniture.* Paducah, Ky.: Collector Books, 1973.

Ketchum, William C., Jr. *Chests, Cupboards, Desks & Other Pieces:* Knopf Collectible Guides. New York: Alfred A. Knopf, 1982.

Lesieutre, Alain. *Art Deco.* Secaucus, N.J.: Castle Books, 1974.

Schwartz, Marvin. *Chairs, Tables, Sofas & Beds;* Knopf Collectible Guides. New York: Alfred A. Knopf, 1982.

Shirley, G. E. *Great Grandmother's Wicker Furniture.* Burlington, Iowa: Craftsman's Press, 1978.

Weiss, J. F., and Wise, Herbert H. *Made With Oak.* New York, N.Y.: Link Books, 1975.

Art Pottery

Barber, Edwin A. *Marks of American Potters.* Philadelphia, Pa.: Patterson and White, 1904.

Evans, Paul. *American Art Pottery.* Hanover, Pa.: Everybody's Press, 1974.

Ketchum, William C., Jr. *Pottery & Porcelain;* Knopf Collectible Guides. New York: Alfred A. Knopf, 1983.

Kovel, Ralph and Terry. *The Kovel's Collectors' Guide to American Art Pottery.* New York, N.Y.: Crown Publishers, 1974.

Schwartz, Marvin D. *Collector's Guide to Antique American Ceramics.* New York, N.Y.: Doubleday & Co., 1969.

Watkins, Lura W. *Early New England Potters and Their Wares.* Boston, Mass.: Archon, 1968.

Popular Pottery

Huxford, Sharon and Robert. *The Collector's Encyclopedia of Fiesta.* Paducah, Ky.: Collector Books, 1978.

Ray, Marcia. *An Encyclopedia of Pottery and Porcelain.* Hanover, Pa.: Everybody's Press, 1976.

Sieloff, Julie. *Collectibles of Occupied Japan.* Des Moines, Iowa: Wallace-Homestead Book Co.

Art Glass

Dreppard, Carl W. *ABC's of Old Glass.* New York, N.Y.: Award Books, 1968.

Grover, Ray and Lee. *Art Glass Nouveau.* Rutland, Vt.: Charles E. Tuttle, 1967.

Hotchkiss, John F. *Art Glass Handbook.* New York, N.Y.: Hawthorne Books, 1972.

Koch, Robert. *Louis C. Tiffany: Rebel in Glass.* New York, N.Y.: Crown Publishers, 1964.

McKearin, George and Helen. *American Glass.* New York, N.Y.: Crown Publishers, 1965.

Shuman, John A. *Art Glass Sampler.* Des Moines, Iowa: Wallace-Homestead Book Co., 1978.

Popular Glass

Florence, Gene. *A Pocket Guide to Depression Glass.* Paducah, Ky.: Collector Books, 1978.

Hartung, Marion T. *Carnival Glass in Color.* Privately published, 1967.

Ketchum, William C., Jr. *A Treasury of American Bottles.* Indianapolis, Ind.: The Bobbs-Merrill Co., 1975.

Silver

Carpenter, Charles H. and Mary G. *Tiffany Silver.* New York, N.Y.: Dodd, Mead & Co., 1977.

Hogan, Edmund P. *An American Heritage, A Book about the International Silver Company.* Angelo, Tex.: Taylor Publishing Co., 1977.

Luckey, Carl F. *Official Guide to Silverplate and Their Makers.* Orlando, Fla.: House of Collectibles, 1977.

Bronze

Day, William E. *Bronze and Sculpture at Auction.* Paducah, Ky.: Collector Books, 1979.

Duncan, Alastair. *Art Nouveau Sculpture.* New York, N.Y.: Rizzoli International, 1978.

Mitchell, James R. *Antiques Metalwares.* Clinton, N.J.: Main Street Press, 1977.

Country Store Advertiques

Menten, Theodore. *Advertising Art in the Art Deco Style.* New York, N.Y.: Dover Publications, 1975.

Reddock, Richard D. and Barbara. *Planters Peanuts Advertising and Collectibles.* Des Moines, Iowa: Wallace-Homestead Book Co., 1977.

Rickards, Maurice. *This Is Ephemera.* Brattleboro, Vt.: Stephen Greene Press, 1977.

Household Accessories

Cosentino, Geraldine and Stewart, Regina. *Kitchenware.* New York, N.Y.: Western Publishing Co., 1976.

DeHaan, David. *Antique Household Gadgets and Appliances.* Woodbury, N.Y.: Barron's Educational Series, 1977.

Hulburt, Anne. *Victorian Crafts Revisited.* New York, N.Y.: Hastings House, 1978.

Whalley, Joyce. *Writing Emplements and Accessories.* Detroit, Mich.: Gale Press, 1977.

Jewelry

Lesieutre, Alain. *Art Deco.* Secaucus, N.J.: Castle Books, 1978.

Mackay, James. *Turn of the Century Antiques.* New York, N.Y.: E.P. Dutton & Co., 1974.

Waddell, Roberta. *The Art Nouveau Style in Jewelry, Etc.* New York, N.Y.: Dover Publications, 1977.

Cameras

Auer, Michel. *The Illustrated History of the Camera.* Boston, Mass.: New York Graphic Society, 1975.

Coe, Brian. *Cameras from Daguerreotypes to Instant Pictures.* New York, N.Y.: Crown Publishers, 1978.

Gernsheim, Helmut and Alison. *The History of Photography.* New York, N.Y.: McGraw-Hill Book Co., 1969.

Gilbert, George. *The Photographica Collector's Price Guide.* New York, N.Y.: Hawthorne Books, 1977.

Klamkin, Charles. *Photographica.* New York, N.Y.: Funk & Wagnalls Book Publishing, 1978.

Clocks and Watches

Bailey, Chris. *Two Hundred Years of American Clocks & Watches.* New York, N.Y.: Prentice-Hall, 1975.

Distin, William H., and Bishop, Robert. *The American Clock.* New York, N.Y.: E.P. Dutton & Co., 1976.

Dreppard, Carl C. *American Clocks and Clockmakers.* Newton Center, Mass.: Branford Co., 1947.

Harris, H. G. *Collecting and Identifying Old Watches.* Buchanon, N.Y.: Privately published, 1975.

Wescot, Alex. *The Standard Antique Clock Value Guide.* Paducah, Ky.: Collector Books, 1977.

Indian Crafts

Douglas, Frederick, and D'Harnoncourt, Rene. *Indian Art of the United States.* New York, N.Y.: Arno Press, 1969.

Frank, Larry. *Indian Silver Jewelry of the Southwest, 1868–1930.* Boston, Mass.: Little, Brown & Co., 1978.

Hothen, Lar. *North American Indian Artifacts.* Florence, Ala.: Books Americana, 1978.

Fewkes, Jesse Walter. *Designs on Prehistoric Hopi Pottery.* New York: Dover, 1973.

Maurer, Evan M. *The Native American Heritage, A Survey of North American Indian Art.* Lincoln, Neb.: University of Nebraska Press, 1977.

Vidler, Virginia. *American Indian Antiques.* New York, N.Y.: A.S. Barnes & Co., 1975.

Sports Memorabilia

Liu, Allen J. *The American Sporting Collector's Handbook.* New York, N.Y.: Winchester Press, 1976.

Melner, Sam. *Great American Fishing Tackle Catalogs.* New York, N.Y.: Crown Publishers, 1972.

Patterson, Jerry E. *Antiques of Sport.* New York, N.Y.: Crown Publishers, 1975.

Starr, George Ross. *Decoys of the Atlantic Flyway.* New York, N.Y.: Winchester Press, 1974.

Waterman, Charles F. *History of Fishing in America.* New York, N.Y.: Ridge Press, 1975.

Vintage Clothing

Allen, Frederick C. *Only Yesterday.* New York, N.Y.: Harper & Row Publishers, 1957.

Brunhammer, Yvonne. *The Nineteen Twenties Style.* London: Paul Hamlyn, 1969.

Ewing, Elizabeth. *History of Children's Costume.* New York, N.Y.: Charles Scribner's Sons, 1977.

Yarwood, Doreen. *The Encyclopedia of World Costume.* New York, N.Y.: Charles Scribner's Sons, 1978.

Radios, Phonographs, and Jukeboxes

Jewell, Brian. *Veteran Talking Machines.* Des Moines, Iowa: Wallace-Homestead Book Co., 1977.

Johnson, Fennimore. *His Master's Voice.* Ardmore, Pa.: Star Publishing Co., 1978.

McMahon, Morgan. *Vintage Radio.* 2 vols. Palos Verdes, Calif.: Vintage Radio, Inc., 1973.

Militaria

Lindsay, Merrill. *The Lure of Antique Arms.* New York, N.Y.: David McKay Co., 1976.

Serven, James E. *200 Years of American Firearms.* Chicago, Ill.: Follett Publishing Co., 1977.

Stephens, Frederick J. *Edged Weapons, A Collector's Guide.* New York, N.Y.: Hippocrene Books, 1977.

Wilkinson, Frederick. *Collecting Military Antiques.* New York, N.Y.: Harper & Row, 1976.

Gambling Devices

Bueschel, Richard M. *100 Most Collectible Slot Machines.* Wheatridge, Colo.: Coin Slot Books, 1977.

———. *An Illustrated Price Guide to the 100 Most Collectible Trade Stimulators.* Wheatridge, Colo.: Coin Slot Books, 1978.

Rubin, Ken and Fran. *Drop Coin Here: The Book of Antique Coin Operated Gambling, Vending and Arcade Machines.* New York, N.Y.: Crown Publishers, 1978.

Games

Fraser, Antonia. *The History of Toys.* New York, N.Y.:

Delacorte Press, 1966.

Ketchum, William C., Jr. *The Catalog of American Antiques.* New York, N.Y.: Rutledge Books, 1977.

Ketchum, William C., Jr. *Toys and Games;* The Smithsonian Illustrated Library of Antiques. New York: Cooper Hewitt Museum, 1981.

McClinton, Katherine M. *Antiques of American Childhood.* New York, N.Y.: Bramhall House, 1970.

Miscellaneous

Bowyer, Matthew J. *Collecting Americana.* New York, N.Y.: A.S. Barnes & Co., 1977.

Gere, Charlotte, and Anscombe, Isabelle. *Arts and Crafts in Britain and America.* New York, N.Y.: Rizzoli International, 1977.

Grief, Martin. *Depression Modern: The Thirties Style in America.* New York, N.Y.: Universe Books, 1975.

Ketchum, William C., Jr. *Collectecting American Craft Antiques.* New York: E. P. Dutton, 1980.

Klamkin, Marian and Charles. *Investing in Antiques and Popular Collectibles for Pleasure & Profit.* New York: Funk & Wagnalls, 1975.

Peter, Mary. *Collecting Victoriana.* New York, N.Y.: Praeger Publishers, 1965.

Revi, Albert C. *The Spinning Wheels Complete Book of Antiques.* New York, N.Y.: Grosset & Dunlap, 1972.

Sears, Roebuck and Co. *Catalog, Fall 1900* (reprinted). Northfield, Ill.: DBI Books, 1970.

Index

Acknowledgments

The author gratefully acknowledges the assistance and photographic permissions extended by the following individuals and stores:

Ira and Mary Lou Alpert, Croton, N.Y.;
Anachronisms, New York, N.Y.;
Annunziata Antiques, New York, N.Y.;
Back Pages Antiques, New York, N.Y.;
Bottles Unlimited, New York, N.Y.;
Donald Paul Brown, Baldwin, N.Y.;
Beth Cathers, Teaneck, N.J.;
Christie's Auction Gallery, New York, N.Y.;
Harris Diamant, New York, N.Y.;
Early Halloween, New York, N.Y.;
Eastbourne Trading Corporation, New York, N.Y.;
East Coast Casino Antiques, Fishkill, N.Y.;
Ethel's Feathers, New York, N.Y.;
Jim Fenner, Brooklyn, N.Y.;
Laura Fisher, New York, N.Y.;
Funchies, Bunkers, Gaks and Gleeks, New York, N.Y.;
Gaye's Antiques, New York, N.Y.;
Audrey and Jerry Glenn, Montville, N.Y.;
Grenadier Guardsman, New York, N.Y.;
Ron Hoffman Antiques, New York, N.Y.;
Allan Jay, New York, N.Y.;
Jill of Story Hill, New York, N.Y.;
Aaron Ketchum, New York, N.Y.;
Rachel Ketchum, New York, N.Y.;
Liney Li, New York, N.Y.;
Eric Marshall, New York, N.Y.;
Myers Ellman, New York, N.Y.;
Nelson's Folly, New York, N.Y.;
The Place Off Second Avenue, New York, N.Y.;
Plaza Art Galleries, New York, N.Y.;
Ronne Peltzman, New York, N.Y.;
Poor Richard's Antiques, New York, N.Y.;
Rosy Cheeks, Brooklyn, N.Y.;
Mildred and Norman Rubin, New York, N.Y.;
Michelle Stein, New York, N.Y.;
Something of Value, New York, N.Y.;
Thatcher Foxglove, New York, N.Y.;
Village Oaksmith, New York, N.Y.;
Waves Antiques, New York, N.Y.;
Charlene Weiss, Massapequa, N.Y.;
Deborah Weiss, New York, N.Y.;
Carlee Weston, New York, N.Y.;
Harriet and Louis Wynter, New York, N.Y.;
Enid and Elliot Wysor, Tarrytown, N.Y.

Special thanks also to Gwen Evrard, Teddy Slater, and Lori Stein.